Practical Tips for Writing Popular Fiction

Practical Tips for
Writing Popular Fiction

A guide to the special demands of
writing genre fiction, including romance, mysteries,
science fiction, fantasy, westerns, suspense,
historical, action/adventure and horror.

ROBYN CARR

Writer's
Digest
Books

CINCINNATI, OHIO

Practical Tips for Writing Popular Fiction. Copyright © 1992 by Robyn
Carr. Printed and bound in the United States of America. All rights reserved.
No part of this book may be reproduced in any form or by any electronic or
mechanical means including information storage and retrieval systems without
permission in writing from the publisher, except by a reviewer, who may quote
brief passages in a review. Published by Writer's Digest Books, an imprint of
F&W Publications, Inc., 1507 Dana Avenue, Cincinnati, Ohio 45207. 1-800-289-
0963. First edition.

96 95 94 93 92   5 4 3 2 1

Library of Congress Cataloging in Publication Data

Carr, Robyn.
    Practical tips for writing popular fiction / Robyn Carr.
        p.   cm.
    Includes index.
    ISBN 0-89879-515-X
    1. Fiction—Technique.   I. Title.
    PN3355.C28   1992
    808.3—dc20   92-7160
                                                                 CIP

Edited by Catherine Brohaugh
Designed by Sandy Conopeotis

About the Author

Robyn Carr is the author of fourteen novels in a variety of genres. Little, Brown & Co. published her first seven hardcover novels between 1980 and 1987, including *By Right of Arms*, winner of the 1986 Golden Medallion for the best historical novel that year. Carr has written two category romances, one single-title romance, *Tempted*, published by Bantam in 1987, a multigenerational family saga, *Woman's Own*, published by St. Martin's Press in 1990, and has most recently added the genre of suspense with the title *Mind Tryst*, published by St. Martin's Press in 1992.

Robyn Carr has also contributed a number of articles on the subject of writing to *Writer's Digest* magazine and taught in the Writer's Digest Novel Writing Workshop for two years.

Robyn Carr lives in Arizona with her family where she has no hobbies and no living houseplants.

This book is dedicated to Nancy Higginbotham,
fellow writer and friend, known most for her loyalty,
diligence and tiresome perfectionism,
and
To William Brohaugh, gentleman and scholar,
who is known mostly for his many hats, his red pen,
and his big ideas.

Table of Contents

Introduction

My son has perfect pitch. This comes in handy if you ever need to know what note the doorbell is. His younger sister, who does not have perfect pitch or even relative pitch, happens to be musically inclined. She sings very nicely; she can stay on key when she's heard the key. She has been taking piano lessons for five years and is coming along very well — she plays lovely music.

My son also plays, without lessons. He listens to the radio and mimics what he hears, duplicating it at the keyboard. Both hands. One evening when my husband and I were watching TV, we heard an impressive piano piece. My husband looked at me and asked, "Is that our girl?" "No," I replied, "it's our son."

My husband listened for a minute and said something like, "Wow. He isn't taking lessons, is he? That's amazing."

My offended daughter overheard from the kitchen and let him have it. "Oh sure, make a big deal over *him* when I've been practicing for five years!"

In the living room, the defensive artist spoke up. "Wait," he said, "there's a trick to it! I'll show you; it's just a trick!"

But she wasn't having any. Off she stormed, huffing, indignant and giving her father the you-love-him-more-than-me guilt trip. Perfect Pitch came into the family room, protesting too much, until my husband finally said, "Okay, okay. What's the trick?"

"It's easy," he said. "You just play the notes you hear."

What my son doesn't understand or *can't* understand is that the rest of us don't know what notes we're hearing. We're *told*. We're *shown*. We're *taught*. We have to translate the notes on the score to the appropriate keys to make music. Having perfect pitch isn't like being a savant;

a savant might sit down to the keyboard having never heard a note and play a concerto. That is genius. Playing by ear requires a model (music), an instrument, a desire and practice.

A lot of writers write well by instinct; it's like perfect pitch. It is a minor gift, a meager talent that without work would yield little beyond knowing what note the doorbell is. Maybe it helps, but I'm not sure it's necessary. It is hardly more than the fine craft of mimicry honed and polished. That's how I wrote my first (and perhaps subsequent) novels. I was able to read good fiction and ask myself questions about the construction— Why do I want so much to find out what happens to her? Why am I on edge? Why does this dialogue seem so good? What did the author do to create such a feeling of desire (or fear, or curiosity, or excitement)? And I was somehow able to discover the answers that are connected to craft and technique, identifying ways in which conflict caused tension to rise; how unpredictable, provocative and clever dialogue characterized; how the emotional impact was delivered me through the actions and reactions of the characters.

I wanted to write. The books were my models, the blank page was my practice, and help books, workshops and articles formed a basis of instruction. It's a very practical way to write a book.

Writing is a field of endeavor in which one small insight can make a major difference. I keep learning this over and over, but a few times I have been nearly overwhelmed by an epiphany-like discovery that more than changed, actually *saved* the novel I was working on. But objectivity about one's own work is hard. Really hard.

As is often the case, I'm better able to puzzle things out when reading someone else's work. When reading a manuscript for another writer I'm more likely to think, "Wait a minute . . . what's wrong with this?" and figure it out because I am unable to fill in the blanks with my mental intention, research knowledge and personal vision of the story and characters. That's the tough part about developing objectivity; your own work tends to include a lot of material that's still in your head and hasn't yet hit the page.

When Writer's Digest School asked me to work as an instructor in their Novel Writing Workshop and sent me a course text to preview, it occurred to me that I would be forced to concentrate very hard on the mechanics of writing, the techniques. I knew I could be more objective, or at least gain objectivity faster, on work that I had not created and in which I wasn't emotionally involved. I thought I might accidentally teach myself a few things by being forced to study the craft in addition to the content.

It was more work than I bargained for; it's relatively easy for me to sense that something isn't working, but it is difficult to explain how to fix it and make it work without just scribbling "needs motivation" in the margin. I found myself scuttled off to resources for advice and answers. I read a lot on writing, gathered a lot of answers and opinions from other professional writers, and nearly drove a friend who teaches writing in a Masters of Fine Arts program crazy. That's when I realized how heavily I relied on my instincts and internal sense of order to do some fairly decent writing. That ain't all bad. But, once you know the technique rather than just sensing it, you can cut to the chase — do what you do on purpose because it works, and works for a practical reason.

Another thing about writing is that it isn't usually helpful to study it before trying it. The best study of writing is a continual process that extends through the execution. Learning a technical skill like, say, developing character motivation can only be learned as it is *performed*. Knowing what it is and still not being able to do it is one of the most frustrating things a writer can face. That's why these insights, these times the "light goes on," happen continually, and at different phases.

A friend of mine has been working on her first novel for a year after taking several college-level creative writing courses. She admitted she was flailing about, unsure. I loaned her my copy of Dwight Swain's *Techniques of the Selling Writer* and she thought she'd been given a beacon to light the way. The most interesting thing, however, is that much of this technical advice had been given to her, at least in part, by her earlier writing teachers. She found that when she was given a lesson and assignment, she could carry out the task, but finding a solution to a problem in her work-in-progress was a different matter. It's simple; you tend to see these things when you're actually looking for them.

By contrast, I tried to read *On Becoming a Novelist* by John Gardner in the early 1980s. I had already written and published a few novels. The book didn't do much for me then, but I went back to it in 1988 and found it brilliant. You tend to see things not only when you're looking for them; you also see them when you're ready. Keeping a collection of writing helps on hand is both sensible and practical. The answer may be there somewhere, and if you're actually writing, you'll probably formulate the right question. And, the questions change as skills develop.

Which leads me to where I wanted this introduction to begin. Even one tip that makes the work stronger, or more pleasurable, easier, faster, crisper, whatever-er . . . that's worth a lot. There are as many ways to accomplish a finished novel as there are hairs on my head; any writer worth his salt won't settle for just one point of view but will shop for the learning tools that are best suited. You'll know what tools those are when you see that they work. Writing can be learned, it can be studied;

but I'm not convinced it can be taught. At least not from scratch. I have a lot of success in "teaching" writers who are ferociously writing and learning. Most learning seems to come from seeking, as opposed to accepting, instruction. Writers probably learn as much from puzzling out their problems as they do from how-to guides.

However, if you know what your question is or where your problem lies, it is possible that one of my answers is also one of yours. I wrote over one thousand pages of critiques for students over the past two years and decided to pull out some ideas on technique and craft just in case I've discovered something someone happens to be looking for.

My plan of action for this instruction is threefold:

1. An explanation of the *function* of each specific technique — the purpose of characterization, for example — and how each technique serves the novel. It's important to understand the theory, why the technique works, before taking on the construction.

2. A summary of required elements of each technique. For example, from the chapter on characterization, you should be able to check the requirements against your own developing characters.

3. Study methods and practice methods to aid in the development of each technique. It probably won't be enough just to read the instruction on each technique in order to replicate it. Study and practice are necessary not only in the beginning, they are necessary for as long as one writes.

By the way, my husband and I found a gifted piano teacher who comes to the house. My son is now learning to read music and amazes us with what he plays. My daughter is moving along a bit faster in her music with the new instructor. After several weeks and great progress, I found out something. My son conned the teacher into playing each new piece as it *should* sound while the tape recorder was on. He is still playing by ear, picking up a little note-reading instruction as well, but now I get to pay thirty dollars a week for it. It's obvious that the amount of energy, dedication, study, desire and practice he adds to this relatively minor gift will determine what he gets out of it. He might be able to play a few popular tunes at parties, have some private and enjoyable entertainment for himself as a hobby or form of relaxation. Or, if he really works hard, he might go on to a career in music.

It's much the same with writing popular fiction. The amount of study, dedication, energy and desire determines whether you are writing for relaxation and escape or writing for a career. That makes all writers perpetual students; the instruction is ongoing and the study never ends.

CHAPTER 1

Getting Started:

Prerequisites for Novel Writing

T here are many requirements to write a novel. Some of them can be searched out, some come naturally, some can be learned, and some can even be skipped. There are a few things — just a scant few — that this instructor considers essential. Period.

A desire to write. Correct — you have seen this requirement in every essay, article, how-to and interview on the subject of writing. No matter how you read it, the four little words are the same. Take just a moment to think about what is not contained in that sentence.

1. It is not a desire to be a novelist.
2. It is not a desire to be published.
3. It is not a desire for a writer's lifestyle.
4. It is not a desire to be rich and famous.

Nor is it a desire to make your own hours, be on a talk show, get a new computer, have an agent or meet published authors. Since writing popular fiction for pay tends to carry a glamorous image of magazine interviews, book tours and talk shows, getting started in this arena for all the wrong reasons is a particular danger. There is only one way you know if you have the absolute right desire for the absolute right thing and that is if you are writing, like it more than hate it, want to continue doing it regardless of the results, and continue to want to do it regardless of the space you occupy, the equipment you have, or the people encouraging you.

So, maybe you haven't started. That's okay. When you start, in that case, look at how much actual writing you're doing. It doesn't matter how much you're doing perfectly or how much you're improving. If you're attending a lot of meetings, reading a lot of help books, taking a lot of courses and attending a lot of workshops *without* writing a lot of pages, it is highly possible you don't want to write nearly so much as you want to *be a writer*.

Or maybe you just don't have the time. Well, if you really don't, why drive yourself crazy with frustration? If your desire is real, and you simply can't find the time, there is nothing anyone can do to help you until you *do* have the time to write. It would be cruel and deceptive to try to sell anyone the notion that you can eventually publish a novel by writing a few pages a week. Good writing takes a deeper and more committed involvement than that. I can't even keep up an interest in reading a good book if I'm only able to digest two pages a day.

If it becomes apparent that the new writer likes the *idea* of writing more than the actual practice, the strain could be too great, the frustration too high, the results too disappointing. If, however, writing is what you want, you can always have it. And if it is a sincere desire, the personal pleasure will lessen the strain and mute the frustration and the result will always be that you're doing what you desire to do. Finally, if you have the right desire, the other things are more likely to fall into place. The learning will be fun, the practice will be enjoyable, the growth of talent will be possible, the imagination will be exercised through use, the intuition and instincts will develop to a greater degree, the determination to get it right will be fueled, and the success (plus those other "desires" — like wealth and fame — that are wrong to begin with but not wrong to discover) has a greater chance of coming through.

Extensive reading. You cannot write books without reading. I'm not picky about the type or the exact number, except that it must be many more than a few. If you have not been absorbed in a good novel, how will you ever know what it takes to absorb your reader? If a good book hasn't kept you up late, I doubt your story will keep you or anyone else up late. And, if you haven't seen what's happening in good fiction, how will you have the first idea what to do? You can read the next many pages about dialogue, plotting, characterization, pacing and motivation, but it will be fairly meaningless without a model to look at — both published work and your own work. If the student of novel writing does not read novels, it is like making divinity on a rainy day — you'll beat it and beat it, but the candy will never fluff.

Many novelists begin their trade as an extension of avid reading; the excitement of reading a powerful book is doubled in the creation of one. Sometimes reading alone is no longer enough.

A working knowledge of written English. A working knowledge is enough. A person who could function as a secretary, write a good letter, or remember their high school English studies will probably do fine. But it isn't enough to "think you know." You better know how to construct a sentence, how to punctuate, and how to use words in the appropriate context and position. If you can't do that, you can't be read.

I was guest lecturing in a college creative writing class and one of the students, a bright and articulate young man, presented the argument that a knowledge of language structure is not as necessary as it seems. He said he spoke well and wrote as he spoke, without a worry toward "rules." He handed me the first page of his short story, which contained a sentence of about thirty-five words, void of punctuation, and three long words that were mutilated by misspellings. I handed it back to him and asked him to read it to me. Reading aloud, he paused for commas that were not there and spoke (properly) the grossly misspelled words. He did not read what he had written; he read what he thought he had written. I don't know about the rest of his story, but he translated the terrible sentence into a proper and interesting one. Problem is, it can't be read until it's fixed. Working his way, his story can only be heard.

There's no excuse for ignoring this requirement because it's terribly easy to fulfill. There are many simple and easy-to-read books available that explain and illustrate proper grammar and punctuation, that explain how to diagram a sentence so you don't dangle your participles or misplace your modifiers. There are affordable classes available in adult education and community colleges across the country.

It is not true that editors "do all that stuff." An editor's job is far more complex, but never mind that. You first have to get an editor and no matter how good your story might be, your novel won't sell if it is beneath the grammatical ability of a second grader and has the handicap of many technical errors. If you take care of this purely technical, easily accomplished prerequisite, at least the reactions when you market your novel will be based on the story, never on the fact that it couldn't be read. Writing to read, of course, includes a dictionary.

That's it. That's all you absolutely must have. There are some other things that can develop over time and are helpful. Some writers bring a fabulous imagination to their work, others begin with a bit of imagination and flex it with practice. Determination is nice, and I believe it comes directly from desire. All those things — perseverance, stamina, intuitive skills, etc. — should flow naturally from a strong desire to write well.

And, there are a few things that will make the work more enjoyable and far easier.

1. Write what you love to read. However simple that sounds, I am astonished by the number of people who don't do it. Novice writers, especially, seem to write stories they would never bother reading. Some-

times this comes out of a fascination with one's own life experiences; sometimes it's just a desire to do something that is beyond the ordinary, something that is not just another romance or adventure novel. Sometimes it's the reverse — a compulsion to write whatever is being published to improve the odds.

An experience or adventure or romance does not qualify one to write a book on the subject; becoming a writer qualifies one to write on any well-researched subject. If you love action-adventure in your reading, don't choose to write a "coming of age" mainstream just because you think your personal life experiences are worth repeating in print. Instead, take all that life-learning into the type of book you love; write about the character's coming of age through an action-adventure plot. Put all the strength, conviction, hard lessons, heartaches, successes, failures, loves and hates into the type of story that keeps *you* possessed.

If you love to read category romances such as Harlequins and Silhouettes, that's what you should study and attempt to write. By the same token, if you don't enjoy reading those types don't be fooled by the length and relatively basic plot line of romance; they aren't as simple as they may first appear. Many writers, eager to publish, erroneously believe they can knock out one of those "little books" to get started in the business. Likewise, people tend to consider children's books or short stories "easy" and a good place to start. No writing is easy; writing books of the type you love to read will be infinitely easier than stepping out of your line of vision.

2. Choose subjects in which you have a lot of experience and knowledge or subjects that personally fascinate you. If you've always been a Civil War buff and you love to read historical romances, you have found a nice place to put lovers in conflict. The research will be pleasurable and you'll feel at home. If you happen to be a pilot and you love to read techno-thrillers, you'll be sharing an avocation in your writing rather than dragging yourself through piles of data that don't interest you.

It is especially important to balance this knowledge and fascination with subjects that interest *others*. None of us quite knows when we're boring; we've all struggled to keep from yawning through someone else's home movies whereas our own entertain us. The simplest way to learn what subject matter readers consistently love is to take a close look at what's being published. Publishers are achingly obvious; they say they want something new, but they keep publishing what works again and again.

When you find the balance between your personal fascination and wide reader fascination, you either develop or reject novel ideas. Robin Cook is a physician and teacher; he writes medical thrillers. Joseph

Wambaugh was a police officer; he writes crime stories. Now, both these writers no doubt have had interesting life experiences surrounding their education and training, their families, their career progression, their material losses and acquisitions and their travels. Those other experiences will lend something to their novels, but both writers found the perfect balance between their areas of expertise, special interests and wide reader interest.

Take a ruthless look at your "special interest" and judge it. You might enjoy talking about your terrible divorce; how many have you enjoyed listening to? Do you enjoy hearing about another's childhood experiences as much as you like telling about your own? When the subject of the war comes up, do you stage a conversational invasion to be able to tell your experiences? My favorite example that mothers will instantly relate to is the birthing story. *All* of us have one; we either fight for our turn or patiently wait to be next. I've never enjoyed hearing a story of a birth as much as I enjoy hearing my own. The specialness is extremely individual. Now, I can put a childbirth scene in a novel, thereby adding some of my personal life experience, but I can't envision a novel about a birth. So, a good test for general interest is a subject that you enjoy hearing about more than you enjoy talking about.

3. Find a writers' group. The learning curve for the new novelist is nothing short of extraordinary. You decide to write a novel and discover that it's much more complex than you realized and that there's a staggering amount of information to be gathered to do it well. Sharing ideas about writing techniques, discussing books that you've read with others, talking about your own writing dilemmas, and learning to give and take critiques can aid the process. Plus, writing is such an isolating experience that just being with like creatures can be good therapy for the loneliness and frustration.

Writers' groups have some pitfalls as well. Some will spend so much time on organizational goals that they neglect the camaraderie they formed to provide. Some spend too much time on workshops and too little time on the social atmosphere that fosters more relaxed and intimate idea sharing. Some groups are purely social and you'll have to add a class or seminar or conference to get the education and training you need. Sometimes the chemistry in the critique group isn't right. Sometimes the area of expertise in the group is different from your own. Here's where you have to trust your instincts and decide if your needs are being met. More than likely if the writers' group or organization doesn't give you all you need, you will still come away with a couple of friends who are doing what you're doing.

4. Consider your time spent learning to write well an investment in

the future. Writers do not like to practice or do exercises. They sit down, roll paper into the typewriter, and decide which market they will sell to. Writers hate to "train." Very few writers have sold their first novel (with the exception of writers published in other areas like short stories, nonfiction, etc.) and I have *never* met a first-time novelist willing to accept the idea they might *not* sell their first novel. In no other profession is this more true. You don't play the piano at Carnegie Hall without years of practice, you don't go to the Olympics without almost a lifetime of hard training, and you don't operate on a dying man without extensive education and training. Well, you don't sit down and write a book just-like-that either.

If you like math, you can go to college and get a degree in accounting after about four years of tough, full-time study. Then you can work as an accountant and depending on the field, your skill, the employer, and factors ranging from luck to the economy, you can make a modest to excellent income.

It's just about like that in writing. If you found a degree program for novel writing, would you enroll? Most new writers I've worked with would kill for such a course. Why not, then, consider your training as a novelist to be like a college experience? In four years you can read many dozens of books, help books as texts, and novels as fiction models, attend many help sessions from classes to workshops to conferences, and stack up hundreds (if not thousands) of pages. If you are diligent and your interest in the subject remains strong (if you don't drop out or change majors), you will have acquired an amazing education at the end of four years. If you're studying novel writing part-time, give yourself a bit longer just as you would take longer to earn a bachelor's degree in accounting while going to night school. You will probably also have one to a few finished novels under your belt by the end of your undergraduate program.

Everyone *wants* to sell their first completed novel, but few will. Finishing at least one novel is almost a prerequisite for then writing a publishable one. The training you receive as you write — making mistakes and actually finding and correcting them — is fundamental to eventually getting it right.

There are different levels of skill just as there are different types of books. Someone who has the goal to eventually publish a 250-page category romance may have to work just as hard as the writer who hopes to publish the Great American Novel. I had to work much harder than my roommate in college for grades that weren't as good. That some people pick it up faster than others will not discourage you as much if you look at your learning as an individual process unlike any other human being's and as an investment in the future that has the potential to bring you years of income and pleasure.

Those four things will make your job easier. I hope this chapter says a lot while remaining terribly simple. To be a novelist you should love to write, love to read, and have a working knowledge of written English so that you can be understood. To make the process of becoming a novelist easier, stick to writing the type of novels you most love to read, choose subjects that fascinate you and many other people, find a class or group to share what you're learning while you learn from others, and view your training as an educational experience and an investment in your future.

Learning to write novels may be hard, but the process is comparable to other career training. Pick any one, from air traffic controller to professional golfer, and see how the same points apply.

Now it's time to get to work!

CHAPTER 2

Genre:

Describing Your Novel

W hat kind of novel are you writing? This is the starting point, the beginning. And this is a big dilemma for some people. But it is so important to know what *type* of book you're writing.

Many of my students had trouble here, in the beginning, even though their novels were well underway. It seems they had stories that weren't just a romance, just an adventure, just a mystery or just suspense. I would persist; I pushed them to decide what it was *mostly*, for a good romance can have elements of adventure, suspense and mystery, just as a good suspense novel can contain elements of mystery, romance and adventure. The difference between types is in the emphasis.

I was often told that not one of those "categories" was heaviest. That's when I would smell real trouble. Often, the student thought that meant s/he had a mainstream novel. What she usually had was a wandering, confusing, unpublishable novel.

Why is this so important? Because different types of novels are meant to accomplish different things; some are meant to scare, some intend to thrill and provide vicarious adventure, some should fill the reader with desire. The *impact* of the story is consistent with its type. Not only will your reader be disappointed if your adventure novel is too light on the adventure aspect and too heavy on the love interest, but you, the novelist, will find your story ideas wandering in search of a home. Are your characters in love or at war? Is your story goal to unite the lovers or stop the terrorists? To write a superior novel, the novelist needs a course to follow, a map to lead the way.

In the beginning, to describe your novel, it is most helpful to choose a genre or genre combination or settle (in earnest, not by default) on mainstream. In this way, if your novel is *mostly* a suspense, you work hardest at developing the suspenseful aspect even as you add other elements.

Genre: A kind, or type. This is very simple yet very important for the writer to fix a frame of mind, a sense of direction, and some basic tools with which to complete the novel. Please note that I stress *tools* in lieu of requirements. Even if you think you have this one sacked—you already *know* you're going to write a techno-thriller—please indulge a few pages. Understanding this part can make all the challenges of characterization, motivation and plot a bit easier, which will lead to a good, clear, entertaining book.

Let me emphasize that this chapter, this explanation of genre, is for the benefit of *the writer*. You must know where you're headed and what you're doing and exactly why this works. Whatever the agents, editors, ad-people or critics call your book later is irrelevant—these other descriptions are about marketing tools as opposed to writing tools. For example, a friend told me that her agent was recently able to get her a larger advance and hardcover (versus paperback) contract by pitching her proposal as "Historical Mainstream." The agent's reasoning was to add importance to the novel, to bill it as exceptional, worthy and of a unique type. Whatever works for the agent. But what this friend is writing, per her own description, is a historical novel as opposed to a historical romance. In other words, the plot emphasis in her story is not primarily a romantic conflict. She is not writing a medieval version of *Ordinary People* or *The Color Purple*. Her story will, when finished, meet all the requirements for the genre she is working in.

A nongenre novel is a mainstream novel—that is, book-length fiction that cannot and will not fit into any category or plot type. Mainstream will defy the conventions of genre. On closer inspection, however, a good mainstream novel does even more than that, and I'll get to that later.

At the end of this chapter you'll find some genres listed with brief descriptions of their types and some subcategories. First, there are some threads that tie all genre fiction together and only in rare cases are these common links successfully ignored.

1. Genre has a plot that requires a resolution; it is not left in a question or a ponderous ending. It does not simply stop—it always ends in the way its particular type ends. In the mystery novel, the mystery is solved. In the suspense novel, the jeopardized protagonist escapes. In the romance novel, the romantic conflict is resolved. (Most of the time the couple in the romance novel will live happily ever after; a much smaller percentage of the time there is some heartbreak, as death

in *Love Story*, or parting of the ways, as in *Casablanca*, but that *is* a resolution.)

2. There is almost always (again, rarely ignored) an element of justice. Sometimes that means the bad guys are caught, killed or stopped. Right wins over wrong in some way if not in every way. There is a sense of accomplishment or victory or achievement. There is a notion of reward; something is gained, learned, won or saved. The genre novel can contain great drama, misfortune, death and heartache, but in the final analysis there is some victor or victory. For example, the detective in a mystery may be motivated to catch the criminals because his girlfriend was killed by them; his girlfriend will still be dead, but he will catch them. An element of justice in the novel does not imply that it is mamby-pamby; even though justice is tougher in real life, in genre fiction there can be great realism and still justice in the end or overall picture. Take techno-thrillers for example—the body count can get high, including loss of innocent life, but the *big* danger is averted just in time, the world (or country, or jet or submarine) saved. Perhaps the bad guys even get away, making room for a sequel. In the end, though, the protagonist prevails.

3. Another common thread is that the type of genre chosen delivers an emotional impact that is consistent with its group. This is something the reader (not to mention the writer and publisher) can count on. If you scare your reader to death with some demonic beast or supernatural being, this could be horror. If your reader is filled with desire, this could be romance. Curiosity—mystery. Tension and thrilling narrow escapes—adventure. Et cetera.

That emotional impact best defines the genre. It defines the tastes and reading needs of the consumer. Some people do not like to be frightened half to death; some people get a real adrenaline rush from a good, spooky, nightmarish story. Some people know they would never dive into the ocean and disarm a nuclear sub that's about to explode, but they find the idea exciting and thrilling when someone else does it and they enjoy the vicarious thrill of physical challenge in their reading.

The type of fiction readers choose is not necessarily a commentary on their lifestyle, nor their hopes and dreams . . . but it is a solid clue as to the type of entertainment they most enjoy. And although it is frequently said that genre fiction is escapist and published for the vicarious enjoyment of the reader (and though this is predominantly true) that isn't saying enough. I have read thrillers, mysteries, romances and historical novels that have caused me to think very deeply on some of my values, belief systems and preconceived notions. Perhaps my social, emotional, intellectual and spiritual concepts have not been as challenged, shaken or reordered as might be from a powerful mainstream novel, but I have been caused to think, I have been shaken, and I have learned. Simultaneously, I've had a good time.

4. Which is another common thread running through all genres. Genre fiction is fun, entertaining, relaxing and exhilarating, each in its type. Entertainment, when used to describe novels, means that the reader is stimulated and provoked into turning pages. It doesn't mean frivolous, meaningless fun. The novel doesn't have to be completely idealistic or unrealistic; it can be quite serious. The reader picks it up with the expectation that it will give out a good time, deliver an entertaining story.

Think of it this way: there are lots of kinds of fun. Some people have fun playing chess, some play football, some *watch* football. All are stimulated. My husband finds jogging relaxing; I would rather practice bleeding than run anywhere. This is why there's chocolate and vanilla. I found sniveling through the end of *Terms of Endearment* to be wonderfully moving and entertaining . . . my husband, the Houdini of the entertainment industry, wants his escape to be pure — the only movies he has ever wanted to see starred Dan Ackroyd. I want my deepest, most sensitive emotions to be gouged; he wants his tickled. That's not to say I can't be entertained by a good laugh or that he won't get anything out of a moving yet tragic family melodrama, but we can only go to one movie at a time. When we choose, we choose our favorite "type." Believe it or not, we're both having fun. Entertainment is relaxation through stimulation. And stimulating the emotions of the reader is the writer's job, regardless of category.

5. Genre fiction also revolves around a central character or characters who are admirable. In the romance, the hero and heroine are admirable. That doesn't mean flawless or perfect, it means characteristics that your reader can admire. A "lead" in an adventure novel may be stubborn, ruthless and unemotional, but the admirable qualities will carry him for the reader — some being strength, courage, intelligence and stamina. The villains in genre fiction are there to be beaten, the protagonists are there to be cheered for. Usually weak points or flaws in a character make that character more likable or more realistic, but the character's assets are stronger.

6. Finally, there is enough predictability of *type* so that the reader knows he will not be tricked or betrayed; the type of story he expects to read is what he gets to read. The reader's greatest expectation (that there is a mystery in the mystery novel, a romance in the romance novel) will be met. Just glancing through the television schedule in the newspaper gives viewers enough of a clue about what they will see by

stating the "type" of movie available. There is enough latitude in each genre so that the reader can have a new perspective and twist to an idea he already knows he likes.

Because I'm a writer, people continually ask me to recommend a good read. I always ask them what type of book they like. Avid readers usually know and respond with a genre or two. Sometimes the answer is something like, "Ah, I don't know, but I really liked *The Hunt for Red October*." That reader likes male-oriented adventure and techno-thrillers and I can add a list of authors that deliver that same type of thing. From that list the reader will develop favorites.

A new perspective and twist, using the tools to press at the edges of the guidelines for the genre (without changing the genre) is the very thing that makes the book special. Failing to deliver the expected *type* can ruin the book. Everyone has had the experience of seeing a movie or reading a book and finding it is not what it promised to be. If you're involved, from the beginning, in what appears to be a harrowing race to disarm a bomb before the world blows up and the story line diverts you to a long, intense romantic tryst that isn't directly connected to the disarming, your anxiety and displeasure rise. You begin to feel confused and betrayed. You wanted adventure and thrill, you got a romance. You begin to skip paragraphs, then pages.

There are special techniques—practical considerations—that make genre novels work. First, review the common threads in genre fiction.
1. The plot requires a resolution.
2. The central character is admirable.
3. There is an element of justice.
4. The emotional impact is consistent with its type.
5. There is a certain predictability.
6. It entertains.

These are some of the elements that help the reader decide what to read; they also tell the publisher what to buy and what to publish and therefore how to sell that book to the public. But first, the genre should tell the writer what he is writing.

When you know what genre to develop, all aspects of the story will begin to hang together. All the "glue" that bonds the story will be appropriate to that type of story rather than extraneous.

Let me illustrate with a practical example. In my first novel, *Chelynne*, a historical romance, the conflicted couple traveled toward a town. Chelynne had no say in who she would marry, but is attracted to her husband and wishes to win him. Her husband, Chad, also forced into the marriage, is sullen, remote, reluctant to show any affection toward his young bride, but is alarmingly aware of her physical beauty. Their coach cannot pass a broken-down peasant cart that's blocking the road. Chelynne finds the cart is transporting a sick child. Chad and Chelynne enter some verbal tussling; Chelynne wishes to help the peasants while Chad just wants to get past them. Chad tells her to mind her own business since *he* is the law of the land. She becomes very insistent, from demanding to cajoling to negotiating. Chad gives in and helps repair the broken cart, while inwardly he is impressed by his wife's strength (in taking him on) and her sensitivity to the downtrodden. She, in her turn, is gratified to see that the man she believes she loves has a softer, more generous side. They are, privately, rather proud of each other and even more drawn to each other, though the central conflict that they were forced to marry and are not yet in love remains intact. The peasants are on their way and are never seen or heard from again. Here is how that small scene kept the novel in its genre:

1. It keeps the couple in conflict together so that the focus is not diverted from their continuing romantic dilemma.
2. It delivers emotional impact consistent with its type—rising desire between conflicted lovers.
3. As they discover new things about each other the couple is brought closer to the romantic resolution.
4. There is (and will be) an element of justice with good prevailing over bad; the characters are not perfect, but they have admirable qualities.
5. It entertains by characterization, brings the setting and historical period into focus, and provokes the reader to wonder if that situation will help to further resolve their romance.

Cut from the book was a scene in which Chelynne, traveling with a maid, stayed the night in a country inn full of young noblemen and their servants. The men were flirtatious and my heroine was possibly in jeopardy, but she escaped any harm and remained virtuous. I frankly thought it was clever and entertaining and it did do a couple of things: it showed period detail, it lent to characterization, and it produced emotions appropriate to its genre—a woman's anxiety over the safety of her virtue. But, it did not keep the reader firmly involved in the romantic conflict, it did not bring the couple closer to their resolution, and it was therefore flab—fun, but not pertinent. It caused the reader to sidestep from the elements that keep the story in its genre.

The point is that faced with a choice of two scenes, the one that develops the genre expectations is the better choice—it serves the story better. Perhaps the second scene could have worked if Chelynne's husband had entered the inn and found his wife put upon by flirts. Perhaps a dozen or so alterations could have given that scene a better "fit." Perhaps if that second scene appeared in the story it wouldn't have hurt the book too badly—it may have been only temporarily distracting. But then the book wouldn't be as good as it could be.

Look at another example. If we call *Presumed Innocent* a murder mystery, all the scenes remain true to that genre. A woman is murdered and the murderer is unknown. The attorney who is originally asked to prosecute the case becomes the suspect. To further conflict the mystery, the love interest in the book happened between the suspect and the victim. The district attorney, it is learned, was likewise involved with the victim. Also, the judge had been involved with her in an illegal conspiracy. All the elements of the story wind back to and are connected to the six elements of the genre. The mystery or dominant question is held central. The emotions are curiosity, tension, worry. The protagonist is not perfect, but has some very admirable qualities—it is not a story about a "bad guy." There is a resolution and we do learn who the murderer is. There is an element of justice (for the protagonist if not all the characters), and it is highly entertaining. In fact, the *mystery* aspect of the story is so highly developed that I often found myself forgetting there was a vicious murderer loose.

I asked a librarian in charge of collections if she would classify *Presumed Innocent* as a murder mystery and she said, "Yes and no." Her "yes" answer came from the fact that it meets all the requirements of the genre. But the "no" part came from the fact that it was not typical. Her "no" part is *wrong*, especially from a writer's point of view. That it is excellent doesn't remove it from its genre and *that's* the point. The book did all the things it *should*. And it worked. That made it special. It often happens that when a genre novel is constructed with this kind of excellence, the baffled reading community of critics, booksellers, distributors and others try to elevate it right out of and away from its home—its genre. *Presumed Innocent* is a murder mystery, *Lonesome Dove* is a Western novel, and *Gone With the Wind* is a historical novel or, more probably, historical romance. I haven't mentioned an ordinary mystery, run-of-the-mill Western or everyday historical romance—these are among the *best*, to be studied and established as role models. You must know about the types of books so you can simulate technical aspects that work especially well.

The writer can become confused in this business of "typing" books because genre has nothing to do with length or quality. The writer must have a course, a road map to follow. Once you are clear on the type of book you're building, along with the requirements and latitudes of that genre, you can carefully construct your ideas to promote that central idea. Only then can you use or reject scene ideas based on whether they serve the best interests of the story. There is truly a lot of room within which to move around, provided you don't move *away*.

Genres can couple as well. If your detective falls in love, it needn't make your mystery a romance. If a romantically conflicted couple solves a mystery as they resolve their romance, two things happen at once. This is one way in which genres can cross and blend and create new categories or subcategories like *romantic suspense*. The thing to remember is that the weight is equal on the romance and the suspense. You begin doing two things simultaneously—resolve the mystery while bringing the couple to resolution. So, don't take your romantic suspense and create a plot of another type in which (for example) there is a child dying of a terminal disease that is not connected in a significant way to either the romance or the suspense. Stick to business. Write one book at a time.

You want your detective to fall in love? Don't drop the investigation and concentrate on love—instead, put a desirable character in your detective's investigative path. Feed, don't starve, your reader.

You can build on what you have or you can build anew, but trying to do both simultaneously has a jarring and ugly effect. You can build a house and you can add on rooms, and all the rooms flow back to the core, the center of the house. People add studies, bedrooms, bathrooms, family rooms and garages to their houses; it expands and beautifies their basic beginnings. But, if you build a two-bedroom house with a kitchen, living room and bathroom and then you add to this house another two bedrooms, a kitchen, a living room and a bathroom, you either have a very impractical house . . . or you have a duplex; you have something else. Most people opt for what works—either one or the other.

Perhaps you have a beautiful but small Tudor home. Do you connect to that original house a southwestern addition? It looks dumb and doesn't feel right. What if you have a lovely but small ranch—you don't need more rooms but your family is cramped in the tiny kitchen and living room. Will adding on to the garage help? Will adding a second living room help or only cause your family to occupy separate rooms for comfort? Or (then I swear I'll quit), if you need bedrooms, do you add them on to the house via a hall so all bedrooms lead back into the center, or do you stack them end on end like boxcars?

You add Tudor to Tudor, southwestern to southwestern; your subplots complement rather than contradict your genre. You enlarge your living room and kitchen rather than building another; you build on to what you have in the way of a story type rather than creating a new, different one. And, you make sure that all your ideas for the novel trace back to the central idea rather than away from it.

A mainstream novel is not just a story that won't slip into a category. On closer inspection it does a great deal more. Good mainstream will challenge belief systems, bring on a new vision, upset and reorder social, psychological, emotional and spiritual values and preconceived notions. Mainstream is a piece of reality brought into sharper focus; it is life made larger than life. It asks questions, causes introspection, shakes up rules and makes them unruly. Mainstream can do that with allegory, humor, drama, diary, epistolary and tragedy. Take a few months to read some Pulitzer Prize-winning novels, some National Book Award novels. You will know exactly what this paragraph about mainstream is getting at. Some titles that illustrate mainstream are *Sophie's Choice*, *The Color Purple*, *Beloved*, *Foreign Affairs*, *The Confessions of Nat Turner*, *A Confederacy of Dunces*, *To Kill a Mockingbird*.

These novels did a great deal more than fail to be Westerns or romances. Also, the purpose of some of these novels directly defied the requirements of genre in attempting to show the disorder of the world, or the injustice, the failure to resolve. They challenged, provoked, enlightened, created new ideas, illuminated problems and crises, presented new visions of old pictures, and did a hundred things.

Mainstream is not defined as better-than-average genre; it is *not* genre. An acquaintance meant to compliment me by saying she thought I wrote "historical mainstream" and I disagreed. She said, "But, if you remove the love scenes and bedroom stuff, you would still have a novel." Perhaps, but if I removed the *couple* and their romantic *conflict*, the story would have collapsed. Romances come in all flavors and sizes; some are filled with explicit sex, some have hardly any.

If you take some time to read award-winning novels, you will have another insight. Some of them are genre novels. The special ones illustrate how vast the range of possibility is in each type. It isn't necessary to confine yourself to a constricting, choking set of rules that robs you of the luxury of inspiring, challenging, illuminating and presenting new visions. *Lonesome Dove* won a Pulitzer; it is a Western novel also filled with lust, love, adventure, humor, history, suspense and mystery. It is full and full-bodied and it does not wander off course.

Many writers feel a sense of relief when they can zero in on the genre; it takes off a lot of pressure because you begin to see clearly which ideas will work best and which don't fit this particular story.

The writer's vision may be large; sometimes the story doesn't fit in a nice little slot. It's an adventure novel, but there is this romantic triangle, that crime of passion, this mysterious being, etc. *Stick to what it is mostly*. When you finally decide, perhaps the mysterious being will be saved for a later novel. The goal is not to get everything in but to put in what works best.

These choices of what to use and what to discard keep the novel doing its job. I'm reminded of a cartoon in which a woman is knitting while her husband is at war, and she ends up with a forty-foot scarf — uncontrolled, impractical, useless. The only satisfaction comes from the fact that the woman did exactly what she wanted to do without concern for practicality or use. She indulged herself in the knitting. No one else benefits from that forty-foot scarf but the knitter. That is not the way to write books.

Work at describing your novel in a simple and straightforward manner. It isn't easy, but it is terribly important. Once you know where the core of the story is, you can string everything off that core and save yourself the danger of contradiction, confusion and misdirection.

Here's how I tried to motivate some of my students to cut out the flab and get to the idea. I suggested this scenario. Say you don't have to describe the novel in a couple of pages; say you just get to write it. You slave over this six-hundred-page tome for two years plus. You polish, work your tail off, market it, and land a sale. The book goes into production. You edit and check copyediting and page proofs. You discuss sales and marketing. You fly to New York and have dinner with your editor. Everyone is excited and sure this novel will be a big hit. And then comes the copywriter who is supposed to write the two-hundred-word copy for the jacket; the copy that will sell the book to the reviewers and the public. And the copywriter says, "Gee, I don't know. I can't really get it down to two hundred words. I mean, it's a little of everything, actually. It can't really be described. It's very good, though, and there's a lot going on." Would you stand for it? Even more to the point . . . would you buy it?

Finding your genre, deciding what it is and isn't, and growing within it are the first important steps. Following are some common genres or categories with brief skeletal descriptions of what they mean. The requirements are skeletal for a good reason — they aren't that restrictive. Use the genre components as tools rather than restrictions and build rather than dismantle your story. In addition to the qualifications for genre, the basic identifying characteristics are listed. Then you must study further by reading.

Reading within the genre is a must; you will find that these genre books range from short, simple stories to broad, expansive tomes.

Within every type the possibilities are vast — there is simple boy desires girl to man pursues woman through three wars and twenty-six years of complex politics. The selection of a genre needn't be limiting in any way. And, it can make your job easier. You might find you have two or three book ideas rather than just one.

List of Genres and Basic Requirements

Romance: Story conflict revolves around the romantic relationship between a man and woman; characterized by romantic tension, desire, idealism and an ending that often unites the couple.

Action-Adventure: Any story line that puts the protagonist at high risk in physical danger, characterized by thrilling near-misses, courageous and daring feats, extremely fast pace, and (often) tension rising to a "countdown" type climax. **Techno-thriller** is a new offshoot of this category, employing high-tech scenarios. *The Hunt for Red October* would qualify as a techno-thriller while the *Indiana Jones* movies would be action-adventure.

Science Fiction: A story line set within extrapolated futures featuring scientific ideas and advanced technological concepts.

Fantasy: Deals with kingdoms as opposed to sci-fi, which deals with universes; story line characterized by mythlike, otherworldly, magic-based concepts and ideas — frequently tied to magical historical settings like the Dark Ages.

Suspense: Dominated by a character in jeopardy, this type involves pursuit and escape and contains one or more "dark" characters who the protagonist must overcome, escape or best. The threats to the protagonist fall into two primary categories: physical and psychological.

Horror: High-pitched scary story involving pursuit and escape most often characterized by supernatural or demonic "beings" that must be survived and overcome. **Occult** category always uses satanic-type antagonists but otherwise does about the same things that a horror novel does.

Mystery: Often called "whodunits," the central issue is a question that must be answered, an identity revealed, a crime solved. This type of novel is characterized by clues leading to the answers and rising tension as the answer is approached, sometimes increasing danger as the solution nears. **Police Procedurals** are mysteries that involve a police officer or detective solving the crime, and the emphasis rests heavily on the technological aspects of police work, sorting and collecting evidence, and legal aspects of criminology.

Historical: Fictional story elements taking place in a factual historical backdrop distinguished by putting characters in important and widely known events, such as wars and political conspiracies, and also putting fictional characters in touch with important historical figures like kings and queens. **Historical Romance** is a subcategory that involves a conflicted love relationship in the factual historical setting, perhaps among historical figures. **Westerns** are specifically centered in the old American West with a variety of plot types from romance to adventure with characters from the time — cowboys, frontiersmen, Indians, settlers, mountain men, miners, etc.

Family Saga: The ongoing story of two or more generations of a family with plots usually revolving around acquisition, adventure, family curses, etc. By their nature, these are primarily historical, often bringing the resolution to contemporary settings.

Women's Fiction: Although not quite a genre, women's fiction is emerging as such a strong "type," it deserves a definition here. The plot line is characterized by female central character(s) whose challenges, goals, difficulties or crises have a direct relationship to gender. This is often inclusive of woman's conflict with man though not limited to that, but also woman's conflict with economy, family, society, art, politics, religion, etc. Romance is often mistyped as women's fiction and vice versa, but women's fiction should exceed the relationship aspect. Many books qualify as both mainstream and women's fiction by definition and description — consider *The Handmaid's Tail* and ... *And Ladies of the Club*, novels seriously concerned with issues predominantly pertinent to women and society — not men's issues — and both mainstream in quality as they defied the genre qualifiers.

Then there is the novel that has women's issues running through it and a love relationship that evolves. I wrote such a book, *Woman's Own*, which I called women's fiction and the *New York Times Book Review* called romance. (They called it that kindly and flatteringly and I thanked them humbly.) There are many romances that exceed the man/woman conflict with a great deal of emphasis on the woman/world conflict and those, I think could be defined as both women's fiction and romance. The only instruction here is that the writer should know when the emphasis of the novel is balanced between mainstream/women's issues or romance/women's issues.

The Road Map

To discover the type of novel you're writing and therefore keep all the story elements pertinent to the genre, the author can ask three fundamental questions:

1. What is the central plot goal?

Is the goal to unite the couple? Save the world from the destruction of a bomb? Unveil the identity of the murderer?

2. What is the primary emotional impact?

Would you prefer to scare your reader to death? Fill your reader with the vicarious thrill of the desire that accompanies true love? Do you want to transport your reader into the adventurous world of futuristic man?

3. What kind of character or characters people your story?

Are you focusing on a beautiful young woman who desires true love? Are you writing about a crusty but clever detective? A bold and courageous secret agent?

When you can answer these questions, you come up with your genre. The description might sound like this: "A bold and clever scientist is transported into the future through his own creation of a time machine and finds himself in an America under siege in the twenty-fourth century." Science Fiction. Or: "A beautiful and shy young woman, reared in near seclusion, finds herself suddenly forced into a marriage with a handsome but reluctant nobleman and endeavors to win his love." Romance.

A tipoff that you may not have set the foundation in the type of novel you're writing, that your road map might be a bit too erratic to get you from here to there, would be an inability to answer those simple questions or the discovery of too many answers. Then it's time to decide which way you're going; you can't go everywhere at once and still pull off a solid, satisfying and entertaining novel.

CHAPTER 3

Characterization:
The People

The proof of excellent characterization is the experience of not being able to forget the character long after you've put down the book. It was only paper and ink until it went into your head. What grew there was a living being who you think about with as much sentiment and intimacy as you would in remembering a long, lost love; or, with as much anxiety and foreboding as your most dysfunctional relative.

There are some basic differences between characters in novels and real people. The goal is to bring the characters to life, to create a truly memorable being. Yet from the beginning the writer must realize that characters in novels are never as ambiguous, confusing or contradictory as real humans. Humans have moments of spontaneity in which there is no reason for an action or behavior; not so in novels. There are people I've known for years who I still do not fully understand; if I don't understand the characters in a novel, my interest fades.

First, deal with why we go to so much trouble with this aspect of the novel. Not to make the story more interesting, though it will. Not to keep the reader turning pages, though he will. The character's single most important job in the novel is to stimulate the emotions of the reader. This is done by showing the reader traits that can be understood, believed and to which the reader can relate. The story line and the setting will not do half the job of stimulating emotions that the characters will. Even high-pitched, dramatic happenings become insignificant events without people. If a car explodes in the middle of an unpopulated football field, you feel something. If there is a man in that car, you feel something *more*. If you know the car is going to explode and you see a young woman with two little children walking toward it, the tension and emotion become greater still. What's more, if you personally know the people involved, your emotional response intensifies again.

Take a second to think about what is happening to you when your own emotions are stimulated, when you *feel* something deeply. You are responding more to your own experiences and beliefs than to the actual event. You relate to yourself as you observe.

Imagine a ghetto scene. Imagine rats, dangerous people, dilapidated buildings, strewn garbage, cyclone fencing and filth. You conjure a feeling (perhaps) of distaste, distrust, fear. (Or pity? Dread? Anger?) Imagine a robbery taking place, a shooter is backing out of a store while firing his gun into the store. The feeling of fear intensifies; there is a known threat — somebody is going to get hurt or killed. Imagine a small child who happens to be walking toward the storefront and potentially into the line of fire. Now there is a known threat with obvious consequence and your tension continues to rise. If you know that child, you verge on panic.

What is happening to you? You are processing these feelings based on information you already know. You've never been shot, but you have felt physical pain and you are aware of the consequences of a bullet meeting flesh. You've never had a child of your own in so dangerous a situation, but you have felt the compulsion to protect and defend a helpless being. It is, in a way, your own fear of being shot that helps you imagine the consequences of the child being shot; your own relationship to being in danger that causes the child's danger to affect you. Our feelings come from knowing how something feels from our own experience, or the ability to imagine how something might feel by a close association with the feeling.

The methods of constructing characters are directly related to their ability to stimulate emotions in the reader. If your characters are passive, confusing or unbelievable, your reader can't anticipate much, can't relate much, can't develop a personal attachment, understanding, empathy, etc. It's like the difference between reading a newspaper piece about the murder of a young woman you never heard of and reading about your daughter's murder. In the first case you react with feelings that are either briefly intense or not intense at all. You eventually put those emotions aside, and while you may not forget, you are able to get on with your life. In the second case your feelings are more intense and your life is forever changed. You'll shoot to write something in between.

There are many technical methods to build characters. My suggested technique builds the character from the bottom up. When I begin to work on a character my first images are usually of a complex, engaging, multifaceted character, but I have only a vague notion of all the events and other people that will cause s/he to become so.

The Dominant Base — Layer One

Working on one character at a time, begin by creating a firm base of two to five traits your character has from the beginning and will continue to have until the end. These will not be the only personality traits your character displays, but the primary ones. These basic, most important features must be carefully considered *and reconsidered*, and must relate in part to the story line. I stress "reconsidered" because when that basic layer of traits doesn't appear to work in your story, the writer must be willing to reconstruct. Even if the plot is still vague in your mind, even if all the details aren't worked out, you still have to create dominant traits that will allow your character to do what he must in the novel.

Perhaps your character has to solve a crime and catch a murderer. He can be strong, intelligent, stubborn, curious and brave. Or, conversely, he could be of very slight physical strength, good-natured, clever and easily frightened but go on to solve the crime and catch the killer because his survival depends on it. The combination of traits is endless, but what is absolutely forbidden is any contradiction in the dominant base. Your character can be weak or strong, curious or oblivious, brave or easily frightened — he *cannot* be strong yet weak, oblivious yet curious, brave yet jumpy.

If you've done a lot of reading, the wheels of argument are already turning. Perhaps you remember a bold hero with a tenderhearted side or a skittish heroine who ran through gunfire to save her child. Stay tuned in — we're not talking about the whole, full-bodied character yet. This is just the base, the most obvious and dependable character traits.

To introduce the character, you first want to show your reader the most predominant traits of your central character because you will build on that base. In some genres it works well to open with an event — in a techno-thriller you might open with a terrorist attack on a luxury hotel. The terrorists might be driven by a higher and more dangerous power and may not even stay in the novel. You will, of course, have to give them character traits that stand out — perhaps cruelty, strength and power. But, when your central character comes onto the stage, the reader's first impression of him must convey one (or more) of his most dominant traits. After the hotel blows up, the next scene might be a ringing phone, answered by your hero. He glistens with sweat; he's been lifting weights. He's given an assignment that's critical to the survival of the world. He is composed as he listens to the grim facts; he dresses in expensive clothes, straps on his gun, hops into his Jaguar and drives, a bit recklessly, to the freeway. He spots a car following him and in a split second after he sees the passenger of the car behind him raise a gun, he puts the car into a spin and tears off in another direction. Et cetera.

The things you show the reader in an instance like this are that your character is self-assured, composed, physically strong, attentive to details and a risk-taker. If he is to actually save the world from the terrorists, he must retain these characteristics to the end, though each of those traits will be threatened on one level or another. None of the predominant traits contradicts another; he does not behave in a way that is self-conscious, easily upset, weak, oblivious or reluctant to face danger.

Complementary Traits—Layer Two

It is important to decide on a few traits, write them down if necessary, but never forget them because the next step is to add further characteristics that can be stacked on the base without causing it to teeter over. As the story grows, so does your hero. He is all the aforementioned things and more. He could have a passionate, sexual side that's an important part of his persona, though in your adventure that side of him won't dominate the story. Yet, in the appropriate situation his lust might lend *depth* to his character. Perhaps in a brief lull in the action he will seduce a woman who crosses his path during his pursuit of the bad guys. At this point it is important to remember that this *additional trait* is not a dominant one—your reader isn't going to see your hero between the sheets more often than chasing the bad guys. It is further information about the man, information to which your reader can relate. And, importantly, lust or passion *also* does not contradict his predominant traits. The way your character behaves during a seduction should support his dominant traits. A protagonist of powerful strength, courage and willingness to take risks and put himself in dangerous situations might be bold in his seduction and show great mastery and dominance in lovemaking. A protagonist of quiet strength, more resourceful than courageous, more pragmatic and intelligent than bold, might be seduced rather than stage a seduction—he might be more tender than dominating.

Other "second layer" information that adds depth will include the character tags—chain smoker, fidgety, speech impediment, etc. Again, watch for contradiction. Does a health nut who presses iron, jogs and doesn't eat meat also chain smoke? Does a composed, poised, strong and brave woman bite her nails?

Everything your character does and says should fortify those dominant traits you began with. When you add complementary traits to the dominant traits, you add depth to the character. If your hero begins as a physically strong man in the beginning, he will be physically strong in the end. (Unless it is your plot intention to damage him physically and you have strong motivation to do so. Every rule has an exception, but the novice writer will benefit from concentrating on what has been known to work before taking on exceptions.)

Contrast — Layer Three

The next step in building character is to show complexity. You already have a firm base, you are busily adding to that base with traits that are *also* important but not *most* important, and now you want to show the human side. One practical way to do this is to show the character's contrast.

You have a strong, self-assured, composed and brave hero. Sensitivity as a trait does not balance well with those dominating traits. If you put much emphasis on sensitivity in him, it will be difficult (read: unbelievable) for him to kill, to risk his life, to turn his back on someone in trouble. You will throw your reader into a tailspin by allowing that hero to speak sweetly, worry about the feelings of the bad guys, or behave (in general) in sensitive, caring, compassionate ways. He is *mostly* his dominant traits. However, a glimpse of another trait that is slightly contradictory can show his humanness, his complexity. Perhaps just as he takes a bead on the bad guy and is about to squeeze the trigger, the villain snatches a small child out of a stroller and shields himself with a toddler. Your hero momentarily cannot pull the trigger. He finds a way to get the bad guy without sacrificing the child. He may even have a thought or two about his own childhood or his own child.

Worked with finesse and wisdom, a scene like this complements rather than contradicts your characterization because the hero is *not* typically a sensitive man, but under the most extraordinary circumstances is capable of sensitivity. And, during his moment of sensitivity our hero does not lose his composure, his strength. When used in that way there is no confusion for the reader to struggle with.

The technique of contrast is not effective until the dominant base and complementary traits have been established, which is why the technique is used wisely and sparingly. It's the kiss of death to tell the reader over and over how tough your tough guy is, yet set up scenes that repeatedly show him saying and doing tenderhearted things. You don't build a tough, intelligent, tenacious heroine and show her weeping; her tears should be rare and brought on by tremendous cause. When you know what primary and secondary traits you'll concentrate on, run them through every scene with the question. Was that strong? Self-assured? Clever? Brave?

I am reminded of a manuscript I read. The heroine was tricked into marrying. Her mean, selfish uncle walked her right into a packed church and down the aisle to meet a man she had never seen before. Frightened, embarrassed and confused, she allowed herself to be passed to the groom. She repeated her vows while feeling like a trapped animal. She didn't turn and run because she lacked the courage and was afraid of the consequences if she defied and humiliated her uncle and her groom. Despite the fact that I already didn't like this young woman, I had not even closed in on the biggest problem—after she allowed herself to be manipulated, forced and dominated by first her uncle and then her groom, she suffered a serious split personality. In the coach with her groom, as they rode through a raging thunderstorm, she had a fit of courage and literally threw herself from the moving coach. She fled into the woods and spent three days in a soaked wedding gown, foraging the plants for food, willing to risk death or at least pneumonia to escape her groom.

Okay, the obvious questions come first. If she *is* brave, why did she lack the courage to run from the wedding? Or, if she *is* passive and easily manipulated, where did she get the courage to throw herself from the coach? If she was afraid of the consequences in the first case (which could certainly be no worse than death) how did she fail to consider the consequences in the second case? Next, the less obvious question. Is a weak and easily frightened young woman capable of showing courage? Absolutely! Under the above circumstances? Never! But take this weak, passive young woman and put her in a situation in which her infant is about to be murdered, and her instant courage might come as no surprise. This ties into motivation, certainly, but for the time being it is enough to concentrate on simply remaining true to the character traits you have developed.

The bride's sudden courage isn't convincing because this contrast in character is shown before her dominant characteristics have been established. Her basic traits were not proven before her contrasting traits were exposed. Contrast only works well when there is a firm basis for comparison.

Challenge—The Proof

One way to help yourself in that effort is to construct scenes (and the motivation for the behavior) that *allow* your character to behave as you have designed. Take our bumbling bride. Alter the construction of the scene to suit her dominant traits. This demands decisiveness in choosing them. If it is to be courage, the wedding could be *her* idea, bravely sacrificing herself as a means of helping a "kind" uncle out of a jam. The groom could be more beastly than she anticipated, precipitating more courage — her flight from the coach. Or, go with timid, in which case her escape must be advantageous rather than courageous. Perhaps she sneaks away from an unmoving coach, before the rain hits, and her traumatic three days in the wilderness becomes a consequence rather than a risk she bravely takes. Now obviously I can't tell if we have a working novel yet, but at least I'm no longer confounded by the behavior of the protagonist. It's a matter of tossing your character into scenes that will reflect rather than confuse the traits you'd like your reader to emotionally respond to.

In doing this, you challenge your character's traits. He's brave? Put him in a threatening situation in which brave actions and words are the only way he'll get out. Is she tenderhearted above all else? Challenge her tender heart . . . force her to forgive someone who has been monstrously cruel to her, in the way Melanie forgave Scarlett. This puts a magnifying glass over your character's traits. When the character comes into clear focus for the reader, the story brings greater pleasure.

To review, these are the first blocks in building a character:

1. Select a few dominant traits that will remain constant throughout the novel and will form a base from which your character will act and speak. This is the consistency of your character, something on which your reader can depend.

2. Add traits that are not dominant, but will complement rather than contradict the dominant traits. This adds depth to your character without confusing the reader. The reader feels he's getting to know your character *better*, not that he was wrong in his first assessment.

3. Show contrast by choosing a trait that seems contradictory to the dominant base until brought out by extraordinary circumstances. This shows your characters are full-bodied and human and gives your character complexity without confusion. *Don't* attempt to show contrast until the dominant base is established.

4. Challenge your character's dominant traits in situations that force action or decisions based on those traits.

I'd like to add a few words to this chapter about characters changing. Many workshop teachers say that a character must change or must be somehow changed by the end of the novel. When understood, that feature can add to your novel. The instruction does not call for a change in dominant traits, however. A brilliant woman does not become dumb; a timid man does not become courageous — unless that specific character change is at the core of your plot. If your story calls for a prejudiced man to have a shattering experience that alters his belief system and therefore his personality, he might move from cruel, superior and relentlessly racist to compassionate, understanding and fair-minded. A weak and skittish man might become strong and brave due to circumstances (read: plot). *If* that kind of dramatic alteration in character is your plot goal.

However, in the usual case, change simply means character *growth*, which is what we've been talking about anyway. The character has important insights that alter his perspective in some ways. In romance this happens frequently—a woman has been abused by a man and is suspicious of commitment and love, but the wonderful hero causes her to rethink that belief, seduces her into allowing herself to be vulnerable again, and proves to her that love can be good, safe and rewarding. Or, the hero is a solitary man who, due to a traumatic childhood, does not trust women—until he meets a loyal, loving and trustworthy one—and one or a series of events alter his perspective and he involves himself in a loving relationship. The character is fundamentally the same; s/he has not lost his or her most basic personality traits, but rather added new dimensions to them. Attitudes may change due to circumstances, but the traits are constant.

Emotional Impact

Those are the first steps to creating characters, but they are still just people on the page until your reader relates or understands or believes, or all three. This relationship between reader and character is an emotional experience. As was mentioned earlier, the consequences of an explosion bring one kind of emotional response if no life is endangered, another level of emotional response if *a* life is endangered, and still a more intense level of emotional response if a loved one's life is endangered. That's what we endeavor to do with characters—make them important to the reader; give the reader a basis for developing an emotional commitment to the character.

Delivering emotional impact is a tall order. And, it's not just learning to write about emotionally charged situations or learning to describe emotions. It means creating the *exactly right* emotions for the particular happening. Sometimes they are subtle. Sometimes a slow tear traveling down a dusty cheek can cause a wrenching in the gut even more succinctly than a screaming rage. For this, the writer must know himself well.

Unfortunately, it is not enough to watch life, to fill up vivid external impressions to be able to deliver emotion to the page. Likewise, it is not enough to couple words well or describe beautifully to elicit an emotional response from your reader. It is a much deeper process and falls just short of recommending psychotherapy for everyone who wants to learn to do this.

The writer must know what brings that emotional response to himself and how that is connected personally, privately, to his own experience. An excellent exercise is to read a novel with the sole purpose of picking up that emotional connection. As you read, learn to recognize an emotional response in yourself. Perhaps something that happens to the character gives you a feeling of rage. Next, connect that feeling to a personal experience. You have probably been in many different situations that brought that feeling. The range of experiences is a helpful study. You might discover you were enraged when you found dog doo on the new carpet; you were likewise enraged to discover your husband in bed with your best friend. It is the feeling connected to the experience, the depth and range of that feeling, that you must be intimate with. Look again at the scene, the page, the sentence, the piece of dialogue that made you feel that. Tie all the strings together—what you felt, the reason you felt it, the situation in the novel and how it made you feel, and your personal connection.

This sounds like a deep, psychoanalytical, personal study because it is. Maybe a lot of writers do this instinctively and don't have to gouge their deepest emotions to capture the emotional impact on the page. But just in case this isn't natural for you (as it is not for me), let me reassure you that to examine your deepest motivations and emotions is healthy, will make you feel better, and will make you a better writer.

I recently read *Seventh Heaven* by Alice Hoffman. A 1950s suburban neighborhood is thrown off balance when a divorcee and her two children move into the only vacant house. All the families (which include one mom, one dad and 2.2 kids) are suspicious of this odd little family (divorce was rare) and remain withdrawn and unfriendly. The divorcee's house is run down and the grass is knee-high; Billy, the divorcee's oldest child, is eight years old.

> Billy picked up the rake and went to work gathering the cut grass. The rake was too tall for him, and it hurt his shoulders to use it, but Billy didn't care. A few cars passed by and although he heard them, he didn't bother to look up. If he worked really hard, gathering the grass into neat piles, then heaping armfuls into the silver garbage cans, he could make their house look just like everyone else's. So he stayed out until dark, and while the other children on the block were finishing their dinners or playing ball or getting ready for bed, Billy Silk was still raking grass, and by then he had forgotten how much his shoulders hurt.

So many things happened to *my* emotions in that short scene. *My* shoulders hurt for Billy. I felt sad and hurt inside, thinking of that little, skinny eight-year-old trying so hard to fit in. The feeling of wishing to be "like everyone else" is such a common thing, whether you were too tall, too short, too fat, too thin or you were the only kid with divorced parents in your whole school. I thought of my son when he was eight years old, the only ballplayer on the bench. He tried so hard not to cry and didn't, till we got in the car to go home. I remembered my own experience with feeling all the other kids had a better deal because my parents started a second family when I was ten; I had a lot of responsibility for chores and babysitting when it seemed my friends were having fun. My emotional memory came into clear focus, the feeling of working so hard to be accepted; I remember feeling that I might be more accepted if I made cheerleader or got a cool boyfriend or something. Well, Alice Hoffman made me sympathetic toward her character because she made me *remember*. I have almost nothing in common with the character or his circumstances. I have everything in common with his feelings.

His feelings. Read Alice Hoffman's paragraph again. What feelings? Creating an emotional response often has little to do with describing the emotions or feelings themselves. It has everything to do with the reader relating to the event. *It was the event of Billy's attempt to be like everyone else that triggered the deep emotional response in me.* I provided the feelings of loneliness, pain and struggle in response to the scene.

It is not enough to take a cool, distant look at emotions in general. If you can't identify what you feel and understand where that feeling comes from, you will probably have trouble re-creating it for your reader. If you haven't felt the pain of being left out (or, if you happen to be a person who refuses to remember, refuses to look at that emotion and experience), it won't be easy for you to re-create it for the sake of the story. It isn't necessary to go into intensive therapy; we are all human and we've all felt all things. If you've ever been afraid, you know what fear feels like. If you've ever been in love, you know how messed up one gets on that emotion.

This reminds me of a friend who was in love. She recounted every nuance of her love, every uttered phrase, every caress, every breath. (I never admitted I was getting bored.) I related to her feelings since I had been in love . . . and on good days still am. Then she made the statement that separates us, for I am a writer. She said, "This is different, entirely, from the usual affair. This is more unique, more spiritual, more everything, and no one has ever been through what I am going through." I realized, the moment she said that, why I can write about love and she cannot. She sees how her state of being in love is *different* from everyone else's while I see how much my state of being in love is *the same* as everyone else's. When you think no one has ever felt as you feel, how can you possibly explain it? If it truly does exist only for you, how might you expect anyone else to relate to it?

The job of the writer is not to invent emotions but rather to re-create existing emotions so your reader can make the connection. To do this you must find the link, the similarity between your emotions and events and the emotions and events of others.

Which brings us to the third step in the exercise. You have found the emotional response (in yourself) from reading. You have linked it to a personal experience in which you felt that feeling. Now, write a scene in which you re-create that emotion by putting a character in a situation in which s/he will feel fear, lust, resentment, sadness, etc. Feel the feeling, as in method acting. Do you remember when your twelve-year-old daughter was the only girl in the class not invited to the sleepover? Remember her pain and tears? Can you write a scene in which a young woman's entire future rests on the possibility of a scholarship, which she doesn't get? Remember the way your husband looked at a secretary at the office party? Remember how you felt? Write a scene in which a woman walks into hotel lobby for a Library Association meeting and spots her husband registering, a young woman by his side. Better still, write a scene in which a man is registering for a hotel room with a new lover when his wife intercepts them. Make use of the anxiety, fear, whatever emotions are involved.

And to describe the feelings? First, the character's actions and words. (And, remember, the emotions of the character will support the pre-dominant traits.) Does she crumble into wracking sobs when he slaps her . . . or does she slap him back? Second, appearance of the character in the situation. Do tears flow down her cheeks, or do her eyes blaze with fury? Third, the internal conflict within the character. Does your description read, "Broken, she fell to her knees and sobbed out her pain," or "Not since she was a child in the cruel grip of Miss Hatchet's boarding school had she been struck, and her insides boiled with fury."

There is also metaphor and simile to describe (of course not limited to characterization, but useful in all your writing). "Her tears flowed as plentifully as the wine at her ex-fiancé's wedding party" is a simile that characterizes and describes an emotion. Or the metaphor "The curtain of darkness enveloped her."

You don't have to go to therapy. You do have to connect emotions that you understand to emotions your reader has had. Remember, your reader may not connect the pain (or joy, or resentment, or rage) to her personal experience, but she can relate because she has felt that way herself.

In deciding what type of book to write, this is a consideration — the emotions you choose to be involved with during the writing. Some of us like the rush of a frightening tale; some of us can't take being terrified. Some of us adore being filled with the passion of desire; some of us are bored by it. This is yet another argument for writing what you love to read. Just because category romance sells so well doesn't mean you're the right person to write one. You must connect emotionally with a "type" of story to pay close attention to the emotions you must re-create for the reader.

If you're going to write romance, you should be well acquainted with and comfortable dealing with emotions that have to do with being in love. If you're going to write adventure novels, you are best suited if the thrill of risk-taking gives you a rush. This doesn't mean the writer must be a rock climber or hang glider — it only means the writer must be willing to deal closely with the emotions involved so that the novel doesn't fail to deliver that emotional impact. Perhaps the memory of the thrill of one flying lesson is enough to draw on to write a great adventure.

Or, as an insight I recently had when writing a psychological thriller, perhaps the best author of a scary book is someone who scares easily. Why? Because I'm well acquainted with fear and deal with it regularly. And because I am not inherently brave, my protagonist *never* goes into the cellar when she hears a noise. She'd dial 911 because it's logical, because I would! When her home is invaded, she doesn't strip down and take a shower . . . but if she *needs* a shower, she takes one with all the doors bolted and a gun on the back of the toilet! The writer must be willing to live with the emotional impact of the type of novel being written. It will be difficult to write a scary book if you are unwilling to deal with how fear feels or have never acknowledged your own fearful feelings.

A final word on the emotional connection. There are descriptions of characters' emotional states that send up red flags and rarely work. "She didn't know what she felt," tells me that the writer doesn't know how the character felt. "She was numb," tells me the writer is numb. "She was confused," tells me the writer is confused. The reader will appreciate your decisiveness — if she is angry, acts angry, does an angry thing, says an angry thing, your reader will get the intended message. It is much easier to successfully describe a character when you say what you mean and mean what you say.

I have a note card on my bulletin board to remind me to be specific.

It says, "I was *uncomfortable* the day after childbirth; I was *uncomfortable* when all the masks fell down on the airplane; I was *uncomfortable* when my mother-in-law cleaned out my refrigerator on one of her visits; I was *uncomfortable* shopping for clothes when the temperature outside was 120 degrees." Words that can mean anything should be avoided, especially when describing the feelings and emotions of a character. Be sure your reader fully comprehends whether a character's discomfort is due to terror or a rash on her butt.

Character Histories

It is interesting and engaging when a character doesn't act in the usual way. No matter how people react to events, we almost always want to know what factors predisposed the action. What made him pop off? How *could* she back down? This is not the "why" in the motivational sense (i.e., "She faced the bad guy because her child was in danger"), but the "why" in the general sense—"She protected her child as a loving mother would, as she had been protected by her mother," or, "She protected her child as a loving mother would, though she had never been protected by a loving mother."

Your characters must all have histories with which you are intimate. You probably won't use all that information and you certainly don't want to begin your novel with a long, slow explanation of how your character came to be the way s/he is. You must know it, nonetheless, and you will periodically use some of that information.

Depending on your powers of memory, your level of skill or your level of experience, you will decide whether you should write a comprehensive character sketch for your own use or fix it firmly in your mind for reference. How your character became the way s/he is helps your reader to *understand*.

"She was raised in poverty by a single mother. There were many times she was hungry, many times she was afraid because her neighborhood was dangerous. She had only one pair of shoes and wore them so long after they should have been replaced that her heels and toes were bruised." It is this kind of history that can justify behavior, illustrate dominant traits. And take special note here, it is a loose justification, and that's the fun. The above-mentioned female could be determined to succeed because of her dire childhood, or be psychologically damaged by it and emerge as a murderess. The impact is that there is a consistent explanation that underscores the character's predominant traits and emotional responses.

In short, you don't just say he's a hothead, you don't just show him acting like a hothead, you go on to say (deep in the novel and at practical intervals) that there is a logical explanation for his becoming a hothead in the first place. And the reasons vary dramatically — there is no formula that is generally accepted for how people turn out. If there was, we'd all know exactly why our children act the way they do (and maybe we'd do things differently, maybe not).

As another example, "He had everything while he was young. His parents were in love and adored him; his nanny was devoted. He traveled, lived plentifully, went to the best schools." The next sentence could read that he was spoiled, ungrateful and never learned to be accountable, or it could read that he was secure, stable, responsible and became successful because of his excellent role models. Your reader generally wants to know (so he can *understand*) why your character is the way he is. Unless you create a history that is so bizarre and crazy that it cannot connect to your character, you can plan just about anything.

Personal Details

Likewise, you should have an image of your character's private life that you may or may not completely share with your reader. You should know what would be in his desk drawer, underwear drawer, glove compartment. You should know how he would answer the phone or leave a message. You should know what foods he likes and what his hygiene rituals are. You should know what bad habits he has and what fantasies he nurtures. These personal items say a lot about a character. Does she keep breath mints and a mileage book in her glove compartment? Does he keep an address book, condoms and a gun in his? Even if you were not to mention these things, wouldn't they naturally be connected to that first base — the predominant traits? Would a woman who is tenderhearted, shy, withdrawn and frail be inclined to keep a Magnum, condoms, mace and dirty pictures in her glove compartment? Never. And don't argue. If your story revolves around an ambiguity in the personality, you'd better make sure your reader understands that. If your story is about a brazen woman who *pretends* to be shy, withdrawn, tenderhearted and frail, but is really something else, your predominant traits will not include frail, withdrawn, etc. Remember, you're supposed to know all the facts about this person. The first person to become intimate with this character is the author.

Values

In addition to giving your characters a history that motivates their behavior and a private life that is consistent, give them a value system that balances well with their primary and secondary traits. If your character is strong, intelligent, capable and brave, perhaps some personal values that drive her are honesty and loyalty. She might find it difficult to tell a lie, even when the truth holds consequences. When your character is tenderhearted, loving, unselfish and devoted, he may have a deep belief that one should turn the other cheek when faced with cruelty. He may find it impossible to stand up to his boss or his wife, even if he feels he should.

Our values are the codes by which we live. They are closely linked to our dominant personality traits, but are not necessarily the same. A value is a deep belief that one cannot easily compromise. It is not necessarily good. A man can be abusive toward women when his belief system is that women are simply not equal to men and do not deserve equal respect or treatment. A woman can be abusive to men when it is her deep personal belief that marriage is a means to an income and no genuine feelings need be involved when she selects her mate. Honesty can be a personal value; dishonesty can.

Although there are many combinations of values and traits (it is as easy for a weak man to be driven by a deep sense of loyalty as a strong man), be sure that the values you assign your characters aren't bigger than they are. For example, if you have a passive, weak, easily frightened man who holds a deep value of fairness and equality to all — will he be able to act on it?

Readers relate very closely to beliefs. The beliefs of your characters, particularly when they put themselves at some physical or emotional risk to act on them, are so personal, so intimate, that the relationship between reader and character deepens.

To develop this intimate understanding of your character, there is a practical exercise. You've gone through the first steps — chosen traits that will allow your character to do what the plot requires him or her to do. You've added to those traits special elements that complement the fundamental personality. You've written or imagined a history that explains how this person came to be this way. You've studied your own emotions and the emotions of the character and are learning how to recreate them. Now, you want to learn how to stay in character and create story elements that work. You can imagine scenarios (and please, write them) in which your character behaves. This work may or may not land in your novel, but it will give you (the author) significant insight into your character and allow you to practice your ability to remain consistent and believable.

Use typical, everyday events and walk your character through some of them. You have a female protagonist who gets up in the morning for work. But, her electricity is off. She cannot make her coffee, take her shower, curl her hair, press her blouse, or get her car out of the garage. Does she laugh this off and make the best of a bad situation? Does it drive her crazy? Does it cause her to react with rage? Take a male character who has promised to help his wife tend to his son's birthday party on Saturday afternoon when a friend calls and invites him to play golf at a special, expensive course. Does he make some excuse to leave the birthday party? Does he become disappointed, angry that he has this commitment to his son? Does he explain to his friend that he's busy and can't make it? Does he come up with a series of hilarious and ridiculous manipulations from feigned illness to a trip to the hardware store to try to sneak out of the birthday party and get to the golf course?

A couple of things happen when you've drawn a thorough, consistent, deep and human character. When there is an event to which your character reacts, your reader will either feel a deep sense of reassurance that the character did what that type of person would do, or will respond with delighted surprise by an unexpected character reaction that adds a layer to the personality and yet does not confuse.

Susan Elizabeth Phillips did a phenomenal piece of work in her clever romance, *Fancy Pants*. She constructed an intelligent, beautiful, energetic and resourceful heroine. When the story began she was rich, and in addition to the aforementioned, spoiled and self-indulgent. But she lost everything. She was so far down on her luck (quite a shock for a spoiled rich girl) that before too long she found herself stranded on a remote, dusty road miles from any civilization. She had only the clothes on her back; no purse, makeup, bankcard or checkbook. She had been steadily learning, on her slide down, that it didn't pay to be self-indulgent and spoiled. She found a lone quarter in her pocket. I instantly wondered how she would use the quarter. Make a phone call to a rich friend? Con some transportation out of someone? I nearly whooped with delight when Phillips made that character stare at the quarter, resolve to change her life from the bottom up, and throw that last link to her monied past away. And down the road she walked to build her life anew. The unexpected twist did not contradict her fundamental traits of energy and resourcefulness.

The unexpected can spice up a character beautifully, provided it is comprehensible.

Here are some of the ways in which a reader should respond, probably unconsciously, to a well-drawn character. The reader mentally canvases one or more of these possibilities, relating either through experience, imagination or understanding:

1. I would have done that in those circumstances.
2. I would have felt that way in those circumstances.
3. I wouldn't have done that but I can understand why *he* did that.
4. I wouldn't have felt that way, but I know why *he* felt that way.
5. I have felt that way and/or done those things.

If you've ever had the experience of reading a book or watching a movie and hearing an internal voice shout, "It would be *stupid* to go into the cellar!" then you know about this flaw of creating a character who does something uncharacteristic or acts on a weak motivation. It's infuriating. The cop whose job it is to go into the cellar to get the boogieman can go; the frail, helpless, frightened young woman cannot . . . *unless* her infant is down there and in danger.

Motivation is another subject. While concentrating on keeping a character believable, suffice it to say that any time a character must do something that is directly contradictory to her basic traits, the reason must be both extraordinary and believable.

I have been talking about *all* characters in this chapter, not just the main character. To pull it all together, when you're dealing with a central character, it is important to do nearly all the things suggested. The central character needs predominant traits, complementary traits, contrasting traits and a challenge to his traits. He also needs a history, a private life and a value system. He needs to behave in concert with all those things to accomplish what he must accomplish.

There are several methods of character development and I encourage every student of novel writing to study them all and find the one (or combination) that works best. One of the advantages of this particular method is that it provides checkpoints — it is relatively easy to go back through your pages and look for contradiction, inconsistency, confusion. "Did I say she was strong and show weak behavior?" "Did I support the dominant traits in this emotional display?" Et cetera. It frequently happens that the most experienced novelist finds errors and goes back through the manuscript removing every trace of a wrong trait and replacing it with the right one. I once decided that a character I had originally drawn as naive and self-indulgent was better off (for the sake of the story) drawn as mean and selfish, knowing exactly what she was doing when she hurt people. I removed every sentence that sounded like, "She never meant to hurt her mother," to "She didn't care one bit if her action hurt her mother, so long as she got what she wanted."

The second advantage of this character-building plan is that when executed well, your reader should still be learning about your character right to the last page. As you stack complementary traits atop dominant traits, add complexity and emotion and history and values, your character is constantly growing, continually emerging. Like raising children, we develop a deeper understanding and more intense relationship with characters as they grow.

How about the minor characters? Depending on their roles, the ingredients are cut to a fraction. The butler can exist on one to a few traits that are not complex—he is pretentious, disapproving, and a man of few words. Whenever he passes across your pages he will speak and act in a pretentious, disapproving and curt way. If you must ask more of him, give him more to work with.

In choosing the people for your story, show the contrast between them by creating different types. Nothing shows you how good a person is as when you stand him next to a real bad guy. Melanie was sweet, Scarlett was selfish and sometimes mean. Ashley was chivalrous, Rhett was a rogue. They bounced off each other like bumper cars.

In popular fiction, genre fiction, the novels are generally peopled with "typical" characters. The adventure novel calls for courage and daring. The romance calls for idealized people whose very flaws become adorable. The mystery calls for tenacity and cleverness. These are not hard, fast rules. It is incumbent on the writer to study the genre and develop a feel for these "types" and see how those people are connected to those particular stories. The connection is to keep these characters "functional." It is somehow easier to believe that a man with some powerfully admirable traits (handsomeness, wealth, good humor, strength, power or passion) might be the object of a woman's desire. See how the originality of the character tends to arrive in the form of additional, complementary traits.

Sometimes a clever novelist will eschew the stereotype in favor of a more unlikely character. If you decide to take a closer look at some of those characterizations, take note that the atypical traits seem to arrive on the second layer. Two dramatic examples come to mind. LaVyrle Spencer wrote a memorable love story called *The Hellion* in which the hero was a reckless, potbellied, beer-drinking windbag who had been married three times, was a wheeler-dealer in business, and was basically considered a jerk by most of those around him. But when his first and long-lost love became widowed and therefore available, the hero, with hope sprung anew, cleaned up his act. He *became* stable, healthy, fit and sincere—all so he could pursue his one and only love. Another example is Tom Clancy's protagonist, Jack Ryan—not a typical James Bond-type, though he has some serious James Bond-type work to do. Jack, intelligent, determined and resourceful (not to mention handsome, sincere and a few other things), is not terrifically brave. He hates to fly, throws up on a bumpy plane ride and most of his acts of bravery are either acts of desperation or some consequences of finding himself in a position in which all the options are bad. He doesn't have a courageous nature at all, but is resourceful enough to get himself out of terrible situations. And he's frequently scared.

The important things to remember about these unusual characters is that their basic traits give them what they need to accomplish the rest. The hellion is sexy and reckless and is willing to try very hard, as evidenced by his many marriages and business success. Ryan is intelligent and resourceful, giving him a basis for getting out of scrapes. The characters are still "functional." And it helps immensely to have some experience before running too far afield.

Just as certain aspects of plotting, motivation and scene construction were discussed in this chapter, so will you find more mention of characterization in the following chapters. Ideally, these things all work together.

Onward.

CHAPTER 4

Plot Construction:
The Plan of Action

The plot of a story is the plan of action. Is the plan of action that the hero and heroine fall in love? That the hero rescues the President of the United States from assassination? Or, that the detective solves the crime?

The plot, or plan of action, begins with a simple idea that is expanded and complicated as unique characters, subplots, setting, action and rising tension are added. So, let's begin by laying that very first brick. The core of the story.

To say that *Gone With the Wind* is a story about a young woman who, through grit and determination, survives the Civil War and Reconstruction of the South partially describes the novel. The plot is much simpler: A young woman falls in love with a man who does not return her love and her pursuit of him creates perpetual danger and conflict in her life.

Understanding Scarlett's goal from the beginning made everything else about the novel credible and entertaining. Had Scarlett not pursued Ashley with such fervor, she would not have been in Atlanta when it burned; her motivation for staying in the first place was to keep a promise to Ashley. Atlanta would have burned with or without Scarlett, since it's history, but it would have had little impact on the story without a significant character's involvement. Scarlett's strong purpose drives her through the entire novel; her actions and dilemmas can all be wound back to her goal; the consequences she faces result from her pursuit of her goal.

The other interesting thing about the central plot is that it would be at home in just about any time period or setting and can be peopled with a variety of personalities. Scarlett *could* have pursued Ashley in 1990 in an entirely different setting and it could have worked provided all the crises, complications and dangers came naturally from her attempts to achieve that goal. She could have pursued him for a hundred pages or a thousand. In New York or Barcelona.

Story Goals

There seem to be only a few reasons for the story goal.

To get something: achieve or acquire.

To cause something: revenge or punishment or change.

To escape something: danger or pain.

To resolve something: get an answer or repair a problem.

To survive something: endurance or stamina.

The Need

A word that should be added to the *somethings* above is *vital*. Something *vital* to the character with the goal. To Scarlett, getting Ashley seemed vital. I never believed he was worth it, but I was convinced beyond any doubt that Scarlett believed it. In this instruction, which for lack of a better idea I'll call the *vital rule*, the goal should match the need. The balance of goal and need to achieve that goal determines whether the basic plot idea is workable.

Goal and need also determine or demand the genre and can often be traced to basic human needs. Consider how the need for safety or escape from danger is both a basic human need and the grist for suspense that puts its protagonist in danger. Consider how the need for love is basic and drives forward the romance. Adventure arises from a need for mastery, to excel or achieve; solving a mystery has its roots in a need for answers, for knowledge.

The drive in a novel hangs in that balance. Consider the difference between *need* and *want*. If a man wants to amass wealth, he should have a need for it that goes further than simple material desire. That need should be pitted against worthy (equal) obstacles. To want wealth for its own sake is not as vital as to need wealth to escape the bondage of poverty that had heretofore been a family legacy.

In a romance, for example, you might find a woman wanting a man. Her desire to win him must be firmly rooted in all her reasons for wanting him. The deeper and more vital the reasons, the stronger and more compelling the chase. To desire him simply because he is handsome is shallow; to strongly desire him because of the almost helpless physical desire, because of all the ways she perceives her life would be better with him than it would be without him, to desire him because he fathered her child adds complexity, seriousness and drama to her goal. And the need grows through the novel—remember that Ashley did tell Scarlett that he loved her, but honor prevented him from acting on that love. (That was all someone as tenacious and single-minded as Scarlett needed to hear!) Added to the depth and importance of the need, her pursuit must be complicated by the many powerful forces that will keep her from achieving her goal. In Scarlett's case they ranged from war to husbands and wives to poverty to wealth and on and on.

Look at a plot line that seeks to cause something. This might be a revenge story. The character's need for revenge must grow from a powerful root. For Sir Trent to set out to ruin the neighboring baron, Lord Southerly, because he doesn't like him is superficial. When Sir Trent seeks to ruin the baron because not only did the baron betray Trent's family, causing all their deaths, the baron continues to rob and abuse those townspeople under his rule. Sir Trent *needs* to cause the baron's downfall to save himself and innocent people. As Sir Trent attempts to meet his goal, tenacious forces stand in his way.

Not many genre novels are woven around survival/endurance plot lines for some obvious reasons: To meet the requirements of genre, to provide an element of justice, a resolution, predictability, etc., more of a goal is required than just enduring, surviving. However, that element is still good grist for a subplot, which we'll get to later. (The survival story is a case in which the major character is usually greatly changed by the experience.)

A character without a goal and a need is a novel without a plot. No matter how fascinating the people in the story are, if they are not driven toward something, they just aren't going anywhere. There is no anxiety involved in listening to a person talk about himself, except in some cases the anxiety of wanting to get away. Without a goal, a vital need to achieve that goal, the tension of desire to see the goal reached, it's a real yawner. Dull. Flat. Or worse—interesting but unimportant.

Vital means necessary, essential or of crucial importance. When developing the basic plot premise, it is critical that the writer has learned the difference between what is important to him personally and what is generally considered important among all people. At the risk of oversimplifying, I don't *care* if Joe finally gets his Porsche; I don't *care* if Jim sits out the entire war in Biloxi. Two (of the many) things that make me care is a strong need I can relate to and understand, and the difficulty involved in meeting that need.

Take a moment here to consider the semantics involved in what I've been saying combined with your personal study of popular fiction. "Need" doesn't always mean life hangs in the balance. "Action" doesn't always mean heads are rolling or guns are firing. "Powerful forces" could be an entire government or it could be the romantically pursued man's mother and ex-girlfriend. When you attempt to make it seem necessary or crucial to the character, remember the circumstances and characters involved. In one type of novel a gun pointed at the character's head is a threat, in another type, a woman seeing her husband in the embrace of another woman is a threat.

The Plan

It is not enough to have a goal. One must also have a plan.

My son is at the age where goals are seldom accompanied by plans. It is a conflict of adolescence. It can be seen in the big picture and the small. It is the child who decides he will be a fireman, but the course is not plotted with the subjects he should study, the physical skills he should acquire, or the attitudes that should be assumed. He sees the end, not the route.

The other day my son and his likewise "goal-oriented" friends had been painting a large poster for school. They had the poster laying atop a huge board. They wanted to know where they could leave it overnight to dry where no one would step on it. I told them they could lay the board on the kitchen table provided it was removed before breakfast. I watched three boys carry the board directly to the kitchen. When they got there they realized that they couldn't pull away the chairs or take the stuff off the table while they were holding the board. They were forced to retrack; they returned the board to the family room floor, went to the kitchen to make the adjustments necessary, and *then* they could put the board on the table. (By the way, it didn't move before breakfast. Another function of adolescence.)

Your plan should include:

1. The type of plot — to get, cause, escape, resolve or survive.
2. Why the character has this need; what makes the need vital.
3. What obstacles must be overcome.

There are three things that make the reader feel an urgent need to see how it all works out (provided the goal is logical and engaging, the characters well drawn). They are conflict, tension and satisfaction.

Conflict and Tension

It's important to understand the why before dealing with the how. The conflict throughout the novel is the only tool that keeps the novel moving toward a climax past the first two pages. The conflict is the obstacle. The many obstacles. It is two men loving one woman — there just isn't enough to go around. Conflict is one good-guy secret agent and twenty terrorists. It is earth, wind and fire; it is emotional disappointment. It is an event, a feeling, an attitude or a consequence. It is everything that stands between your protagonist and his/her meeting a fundamental need and reaching a goal. That vital "something" must be difficult to get, cause, escape, resolve or survive.

First, there must be the central conflict, the most obvious obstruction. Your hero, though skilled and brave, faces terrible odds in his quest to overcome a group of terrorists. Or, your heroine is impossibly drawn to a man who does not return her love. Or, there is a serious crime that must be solved to prevent further such crimes and a minimum of clues available. That's information the reader wants to know at the very beginning. The reader first wants to know what the goal is, next told why the need is great, then immediately be shown why this is not going to be easy.

Next, each subsequent conflict must be somehow related to that central one. Your hero cannot overcome the terrorists because he doesn't know where they are. When he looks for them, a traitor gives him erroneous information. When he overcomes that and gets the right information, he finds himself intercepted and in danger. When he gets out of that and continues his pursuit, he finds he is too late to stop yet another terrorist mission. And so on.

Our love-stricken heroine? First she wants a man who does not want her. Then when he begins to respond to her she learns that as a result of a failed love affair he no longer trusts women. When trust begins to build, his ex-girlfriend returns and he is now torn between the old love and the new. When the ex-girlfriend turns out to be an opportunist who had not returned to him out of love but rather out of a need for money, he finds out too late—after actually marrying her. And so on. Each time she (or they) resolve one conflict, another arises until all the obstacles have been successfully passed and they either live happily ever after or part. (But there *is* a resolution.)

Conflict not only must come and go throughout the story, it also must be tied to the plot and characters; it must be pertinent. When a conflict or one of the obstacles is not related to the basic plot, it fails to cause the rising tension and anxiety of the reader. It lacks urgency because the goal and need change. If your hero is assigned the task of finding and eliminating a group of terrorists, his goal will not be complicated by a phone call from his mother telling him his brother has AIDS. He may be diverted (as the reader will be), or stalled, or sidetracked, or delayed. A conflict that has nothing to do with the plot line causes the story to take a left turn because the ill-fitting conflict does not lead toward achieving the goal even if it does in some way impact the character.

Novels become really fun and interesting when the author employs every available and reasonable source for both anticipated and unexpected conflict. In *Gone With the Wind* the Civil War became more than just a setting when events of the war continually complicated Scarlett's efforts to get Ashley. And Scarlett likewise used the war as a means to attract Ashley. That would account for some "anticipated" conflict. The reader can guess that if Scarlett gets near a city that is going to be pulverized, she'll be in danger.

On the other hand, there were unexpected conflicts. I did not expect Melanie to forgive and embrace Scarlett after Scarlett had attempted to seduce Ashley. I didn't expect Scarlett's child to die suddenly and put an end to Rhett's tolerance.

A clever writer makes use of this technique by alternating the anticipated and unexpected conflicts. There should be a warning label on this technique, however. No trickery allowed. You are responsible for knowing that unexpected event is coming. In *Gone With the Wind* there was no clue of Scarlett's daughter's death, but what had been established was Rhett's growing impatience and his proclamation that his child was so important to him that he insisted Scarlett behave as a wife and mother should. The reader, therefore, could anticipate that without the child their relationship would fall apart. Also, Mitchell introduced the pony from which the child would fall before the scene in which the child is killed — using the old rule, if you introduce a gun, fire it. The child's death was a shock, the reaction was surprise, but all the elements leading to it were reasonable and believable.

As another example, your techno-hero may encounter the completely unexpected conflict of learning that his most trusted friend is actually on the enemy's side, but the groundwork must be solid. You must build in some opportunity for the "friend" to have functioned as a traitor. I'm not saying that you tip-off your reader, just that you remain consistent. Build the friendship and trust, but remember that if the "friend" is on the other side, he will not help the hero beat him. If he's working for the enemy, perhaps he is unavailable when needed and his whereabouts are mysterious, his excuses suspicious. When the reader learns the truth, the reader can either go back through the book or remember passages that make the surprise revelation plausible. When the traitor is exposed your reader should not remember any story detail that would dispute that fact.

Tension and Consequence

If the conflicts are plausible and appropriate, the reader's tension level increases. The character gets closer and closer to his/her goal, but the stakes get higher with each step. For the sake of tightening the tension or the urgency to get to the end of the story, there has to be an important reason why the stakes are higher—and that reason is closely tied to consequence. There might be a time constraint—perhaps the button has been pushed, the bomb launched, and the hero has a limited time period in which to achieve his goals. Or perhaps the opposition is gaining strength. Whatever, because of time running out, the protagonist is in a hurry and under pressure.

Perhaps the consequence is increasing destruction. In a mystery or police procedural the killer may be getting a high body count and every moment the detective (or investigator or sleuth) delays, more lives could be lost. Sometimes the consequence is increased risk to the protagonist; every time a woman fails to escape the assailant the possibility of her own demise draws nearer.

In romance, the consequence is often increased emotional damage. When our heroine first noticed the hero and was drawn to him, her desire for him was strong but not desperate. Had he left the country at that moment and was never seen again, she wouldn't have much trauma in overcoming her feelings for him. But with each touch, each kiss, each deepening understanding, and of course *his* response that propels rather than kills off her pursuit, her desire grows apace. As the story grows, so does her involvement until the romantic conflict reaches a point where for her to lose will cause a badly broken heart. At this point, to lose would be devastating.

So, the writer raises the stakes; the foe gets more dangerous, the time is running out, the need is increasing, the consequences of not reaching the goal become more and more dire. The novel gets very exciting when the author brings the conflict and the tension to the breaking point.

Tension and Satisfaction

And what about the satisfaction factor? This is not simply what happens at the end, when the hero wins or the lovers unite. Satisfaction occurs throughout the novel in what Dwight V. Swain (*Techniques of the Selling Writer*) describes, at great length, as scene and sequel. Briefly, it is the technique of following a major event (major conflict, action and reaction) with a slight cooling off period in which the conflict is further examined and the next one is set up. It is the technique of increasing the intensity of the conflict, letting the protagonist make some progress toward his/her goal and then throwing another obstacle in his/her path. Your techno-hero gets the correct directions to the headquarters and voilà! He finds the hideout. He moves in. But he is too late—they are gone and he has failed to stop another terrorist attack. He must retrack and retrench. He must come up with a new (subsequent) plan.

Another example. Our romance heroine is getting closer to satisfaction. She not only has heard her hero's admission of love, he's demonstrated it. He takes her in his arms and speaks all the words of passion. He takes her to bed; he tells her he has never been so in love and never will be again. And after all this passion (which is better passion than the best passion in the whole world) he makes his confession. While he will always love her desperately, he can never marry her. He is a Catholic priest.

It has a little bit of a "boom-chuckaluckalucka-boom-chuckaluckalucka" rhythm to it. There is conflict, action, reaction. Then again, conflict, action, reaction. Every barrier crossed brings a new barrier to be crossed. Between barriers, while problems are assessed and new plans are laid, the reader gets a sense of satisfaction from the progress and the relief that the last crisis was resolved or survived or surpassed. Just when our heroine got the man of her desires to admit his own feelings, he came up with yet another barrier for her to hurdle. The tension is rising and falling, but each rise is greater than the last and the whole wave is moving toward the final conclusion.

Caution: The obstacles that stand in the way are new ones. Backsliding can slow down and damage your story line. To have a man express his love and then withdraw it and then reconsider and express it again makes him appear confused and befuddled. To have a man express his love but reveal that the next obstacle is his priesthood provides a new conflict, it doesn't re-create an old one. This keeps the writer from doing and undoing the story.

Lining It Up

Good organization and the ability to revise and rewrite provides essential glue to the plot. Obviously every detail of the story is not crystal clear when working on page one, but there must be a strong skeleton—the basic plot and fundamental character traits. Then, when you develop a conflict, an obstacle for your protagonist to face, be prepared to return to earlier portions of the manuscript and revise so that the obstacle is set up and doesn't appear to come out of the blue. For example, you plan to complicate your romantic heroine's pursuit of the hero by bringing in another woman to compete. That woman has existed, even if she wasn't on the scene. There must be some indication of her early on. It need not be a huge buildup; it may be a simple sentence or two. The hero could say, "I married ten years ago. After three years of marriage my wife left me and I haven't seen her or talked to her since." Then in chapter seven a woman shows up—the ex-wife? No. The *wife*. He didn't mention they never bothered to divorce.

When you attempt to organize your conflicts, be reasonable in your expectations of the reader. I had a heroine who was a single mother of two small children. Her means were slim when her house burned down. It was my plan for the hero to step in and help her, care for her, and eventually fall in love with her. It was my further plan to complicate this romance by having the heroine *appear* to be destitute when in fact she was estranged from an extremely wealthy family . . . a family she did not wish to be reunited with and therefore would not ask for help. It was reasonable for her to decide to conceal her personal history from the hero when she'd only just met him. But *she* knew her own personal history. It was not reasonable for her not to even think about it. It was not credible for her to see the hero's house and gasp in awe over his nice furnishings when hers had once been even more luxurious. Therefore, she thought about her past, the reader knew a few details about it, and the hero was still shocked by the information when it came.

Another surprise conflict I had to retrench to set up was my heroine's rich aunt. I decided the story would be a lot more interesting if the rich, old bat were actually only twelve years older than the heroine, and classy to boot. Then I decided it would be still more interesting if the hero assumed the aunt was an old bat. I went back to the beginning to delete a description of an old woman and add allusions to the woman being a crotchety old bat, to mislead other characters. "I call her my old maid aunt because she hasn't married," the heroine said. "She's impossible; she's so set in her ways." When Aunt Flo steps off the plane and is a forty-year-old knockout, the reader might get a kick out of the surprise impact this has on the other characters, but I wouldn't dare mislead the reader. When the heroine thought of her aunt, she thought of her accurately and clearly.

Then there was (I hope) a real shock for the reader. When my heroine, who worked as a grocery checker, was ringing up sales, she saw her own face stare back at her from the front of a tabloid with the headline, "The Missing Heiress." I did nothing to prepare the reader for the headline, but I did plenty to prepare the reader for its possibility by establishing the heroine as formerly wealthy, divorced from a con man, and estranged from her family.

Being well organized in delivering information and planning credible surprises for your reader has a strong connection to the tension-building aspect of conflict. You already know you want the reader to want a question answered; be sure you give your reader the right question. It is usually easier to build tension by *giving* information rather than withholding it. Not telling enough can build confusion rather than tension.

I made that very mistake in a prologue that I worked and reworked for months. No matter how the novel grew, I kept going back to that prologue with a hunch something was wrong. It was a scene in which a woman in a poor neighborhood was giving birth with the help of a midwife. I wanted the reader to "guess" that the woman had been reduced from wealth to poverty; I went to a great deal of trouble to describe how it *confused* the midwife that the young mother had no furniture but had cut up expensive dresses for window coverings. She sewed a ratty-looking blanket, but had not tried to make clothes for her child. She had no pots, but she had combs and lace underthings. I tried every manipulation until I found the one thing that worked. What worked was saying it—the midwife was not confused but *aware* that the young mother must have been a rich girl reduced to poverty; all the above items spelled it out. (This reaches back to characterization; a confused character seldom tells your reader anything important.) Organizing your story facts, material and information can create the right question. In the above example the question changes from "What's going on?" to "How did this poor woman suffer such a dramatic loss of lifestyle?" From "What's happening?" to "How did that happen?" (Need I stress that "What's going on here?" is never a good reader question?)

Every time you think along the lines of, "I want the reader to wonder if he's hiding something," or "I want the reader to wonder where she came from," just consider telling the reader what he's hiding or where she came from. See if it doesn't work.

Subplots

A subplot is another small story that is running alongside the central plot. The characters in the subplot have direct involvement with both the central character(s) and the central plot; their actions and conflicts can affect the outcome of the main plot. How complex or how simple this second (and in some cases third or fourth) story is has many variables and only one rule: It must not overshadow the central plot in time, space or importance.

The subplot has many practical functions. Let me illustrate with a simple example. I read a short, lovely romance in which the heroine was the single mother of an asthmatic child. The presence of the child frequently complicated the actions of the lovers—they were interrupted, prevented from being alone together and at times the boy had to come first because of his needs. An asthma attack provided a real crisis/emergency during which the couple had to ignore their own needs/desires and function as responsible adults. Finally, because of her son's condition, the heroine had to make a hard choice—watch her son suffer so she could be near her true love or move to another climate with her child.

The story goal was to get the man and woman together. In that case the subplot provided further conflict, caused tension to rise, and ultimately helped to characterize the hero and heroine by showing more aspects of their personalities as they related to the child. The heroine's devotion and unselfish caretaking caused the hero to admire her even more; the hero's ability to communicate with the child in a gentle and fatherly way made the heroine hopeful.

Another practical and entertaining function of a subplot is to give the author the opportunity to solve one problem at a time and provide more than one resolution. I've found this to be a great asset in writing romance when my conflicted couple has more than one problem. It's romance, so of course the major problem is getting them together. But, there is another threat—perhaps a dark knight who wants to kill the white knight. It's a treat to get the couple together, allow the reader to enjoy their togetherness, and watch them unite to resolve the final conflict as a couple. It's reassuring. There is still the pressure of trouble to be resolved, but thank goodness that man and woman are solidly together.

The subplot helps give a new dimension to the plot type (so long as it doesn't change the basic plot), when it's of a different type. As was discussed in the chapter on genre, your detective can have a love interest, but it must be a part of his/her investigation. Your techno-hero might have a family crisis, but that crisis must be part of the central plot—perhaps his son is kidnapped by the terrorists or his wife is threatened. It is often a love interest that adds dimension to the opposite-type plot—during a lull in the adventure/suspense/mystery, man and woman are drawn together, the author careful not to put more emphasis on the romance than the larger question.

The subplot can also add depth and complexity to the plot and characters when it's the same type. In my first romance the hero was struggling to regain control of his usurped family lands (simultaneously resolving the romantic conflict with the woman he desired). His best friend, also a nobleman, was helping him. The best friend, while working on the problem of getting back the land, fell in love with a local peasant girl. The best friend's romance ran alongside the hero's romance neck in neck; the friend's romantic conflicts were different from the hero's, but because it was a nobleman and peasant girl from the community, it affected the total outcome of the story.

Plotting Is Thinking

When you consider it, there are just a few essential components to plotting: All you need is a goal, a need to achieve that goal, a plan of action, a lot of cause and effect, action and reaction, and enough obstacles in pursuit of the goal to create conflict and cause the reader's anxiety level to rise (tension). And of course a culmination, a resolution, an ending in which the plan comes together and the goal is reached, the problem solved, the question answered. It's probably less complex than characterization; it's a simpler process to execute a plan than to create a complex and multifaceted character with whom your reader will relate, who your reader will understand and believe.

That's the good news. The bad news is, plotting is the hardest part for most writers. It must be. Not only is it harder for me than any other aspect of the novel, I've read some excruciatingly bad novels lately that indicate it's hard for others.

One difficulty is that a great plot requires a great idea at its core. Even worse than that, it requires many more exceptional ideas to support the plot and drive it forward. And now if you think I can give you the formula for coming up with great ideas, you've just reached your third disappointment in one paragraph. For me, as for so many, getting the single, solid central idea (and all the complementary spin-off ideas that support and drive it forward) is torture. I'd rather have a root canal. When I'm asked that question — Where do you get your ideas? — as I am at every gathering where they know I'm a writer — I want to respond, "How the hell do I know?"

Because I search for them, and the search is strenuous. I don't dream them or have them "come" to me. There is only one method I've come up with that works for me. I think. And think. And think harder. When I see the faintest mirage of an idea, I test it against all the things that can possibly go wrong. I wrestle it to the ground and pin it — often it slips away from a choke hold. I punch and stab it and try to tie it down. I pounce on it and shake it into place; it often wriggles away. I stop the writing and read, pace, think, throw in some laundry, clean a toilet, pace some more. Sometimes I try ideas out on friends — special friends, the ones who tend to question everything and aren't easily satisfied. Occasionally one idea seems to flow into the next, but this is rare. Most of my novels have five endings to choose from because just when I think it's okay, I realize it isn't. I say "not good enough" one hundred times more often than I say "there!"

The ideas I reject are any that would not satisfy me as a reader— problems with logically simple solutions (even though I could create a character dumb enough not to see it); improbable conflicts in which a simple misunderstanding could be resolved with some dialogue. Anything that is convenient, coincidental or unlikely goes out the window. The writer, the plotter, becomes the problem solver. The more difficult the problem, the more difficult the solution, the better the plot idea.

You can sniff out workable ideas from reading fiction, and I'll talk more about how to study fiction in chapter nine. You know the idea is workable (the core idea) when it's worked on you and many other readers. You know that "boy gets girl" works, and through study you'll be able to tell whether "man risks losing a huge inheritance to marry a poor girl" works better than "man risks offending his mother by marrying against her wishes" by doing your own comparison. The impact the idea has on you is the first test; the impact the idea has on the world is the second.

Pitfalls

And then so much can still go wrong, even when you attempt to run it through your checklist. Some of the reasons this is so difficult to do will come into focus by looking at some of the most common pitfalls.

For new writers, especially, the thing that goes wrong most often is not having a plot idea at all or an idea too vague and slippery. This seems to come from plain old inexperience and not enough information on how to discover what plot *is*. It comes from lack of practice in separating the components of the novels one is reading. Plot is the plan of action—the difference between Scarlett as a woman who survives the Civil War and Scarlett as a woman in pursuit of a man who does not return her love.

Experienced readers and reviewers comment on strong plot, weak characterization; believable plot lines versus unbelievable ones. Here's one way to study plot. Pick a title, preferably a popular hardcover since it would be more widely reviewed. This process is easier if you choose a book that is widely praised and you also enjoy. Read the book jacket description first, then begin to study the reviews. Your library is an ideal place—you can find reviews in many periodicals including *Library Journal, Kirkus, Publishers Weekly*, and the *New York Times Book Review*.

The reviewers will have a lot to say about the book, what they think works and what doesn't, but try to gather from the reviews and jacket what the book is about—what question the reader is expected to ask himself.

"*Night of the Ice Storm* by David Stout, (Mysterious Press/Warner, $19.95). Nature goes on a rampage in this coolly terrifying novel set in upstate New York, unleashing in one person the passion for murder." I haven't read the novel, but I bet the question is either "who is the killer?" or "will he be caught?" I promise the question is not "what kind of storm?" or "where in upstate New York?"

This is an excerpt from the jacket of *The Servants of Twilight* by Dean R. Koontz: "An ordinary parking lot in Southern California. Christine Scavello and her six-year-old son are accosted by a strange old woman. 'I know who you are,' she snaps at the boy. 'I know *what* you are.' A scream, a threat—and then a grotesque act of violence. Suddenly Christine's only son is targeted by a group of religious fanatics. They've branded him the Antichrist. They want to kill him. And they are everywhere. . . . "

Several questions about the scenario come to mind, but the central question is "Will they get the boy?" That question then runs through the novel from beginning to end as Christine and her son flee from the group of fanatics. There are certainly other questions: "How did the group choose the boy?" "Will anyone else be killed?" etc. But the central question is asked as each new conflict puts the boy in jeopardy. And note: By the information given on the jacket, we know the question is *not* "Why are they after the boy?" We know why.

In reading reviews, jackets and then the entire novel, ask yourself these three questions:

1. What, specifically, do I *most* want to know?

Do you want to know if the religious fanatics will get the boy, or if the boy's mother and the detective who is helping her will fall in love? Do you most want to know if the man and woman will find true love, or if the woman's mother is really a terrible gossip? Do you want to know if the hero will be able to disarm the bomb before the thing blows, or do you want to know if he's going to fall in love with the scientist who's helping him?

2. Who, specifically, is at greatest risk in the story?

Is it the boy who has had attempts made on his life, or the leader of the cult? Is it the heroine who loves so deeply, devotedly, in constant fear that the object of her desire will not return her love, or is it the friend who is advising her? Is it the techno-hero who, with only seconds left, attempts to disarm the bomb, or is it the scientist who radioed him the instructions?

3. In the resolution of the story, what question was finally answered?

Did the boy get killed or get away? Did the woman win the man's love? Did the techno-hero disarm the bomb? Did the detective discover who the murderer was?

The answer to those three questions gives you the actual plot. "The boy, targeted as the Antichrist by a group of religious fanatics, flees with his mother and a private detective. After many close calls and several deaths to those helping them escape, the leader of the cult is captured, killed and the boy escapes."

Before you can plot, you will have to be certain what a plot is. If you don't have it yet, keep studying fiction until you get it.

Another pitfall is a contrived story idea—gold spun out of straw. Just too ordinary, convenient and weak to sustain tension, to cause the reader anxiety that prompts page-turning. This frequently comes from building the big obstacle and the big consequence out of something that just doesn't strike the reader as that serious, that vital. Like a family in a haunted house when there is no clear or vital reason why they just can't bug out to a Holiday Inn. But have their youngest child sucked into the TV by spooks and now they stay to get her back.

Or, the goal and need can be real enough but the obstacle is contrived. An editor I know once said, "Don't give me any problems I can resolve with a phone call." *Can* is the key word; if your hero walks right past a phone into a burning building instead of calling the fire department, your reader is at least as smart as you are. Your reader knows that was convenient, stupid on the part of the character, and that the writer created this action arbitrarily. He *could* have called for help. So why didn't he? It is often because the writer needed him in the burning building. Not a good enough reason. But, he has no quarter for the phone and his best friend is tied up in there, and the need becomes more immediate.

I read an entire novel in disbelief—the plot revolved around information the heroine's mother knew but didn't want to discuss. I read on—surely she wouldn't do it, she wouldn't construct an entire plot around this information; she wouldn't finally share the critical information, after months (and pages) of conflict, and at the last moment allow the mother to breathe a sigh of resignation and let it out, finally allowing the heroine to achieve her goal. But yes. She did. The heroine had asked her mother a critical question about the mother's past in the beginning of the novel; the mother had said, "I don't want to discuss it." Heroine respected mother's wishes. She didn't pry or insist until her very life hung in the balance. In *what* family, I ask you? Not mine. No one gets to keep a secret long around here; we are as tenacious as bulldogs. If the heroine in the above case had needed that information, she should have attained it and had another, stronger obstacle to her success. Or, her mother should have been dead and unable to answer the question.

Another thing that can go terribly wrong is to get the *facts* wrong. This is complicated — it's every little fact. The plot falls apart and credibility is out the window when you give the wrong information. Although this is fiction, you can't make everything up as you go along, particularly in fact-intensive genre fiction such as techno-thrillers, science fiction, police procedurals and historical fiction. The audience for such books is well informed.

Erroneous facts slip through because of laziness — just plain not looking harder for the right information. Another reason is lack of diligence — taking the first answer you get from a secondary source because it fits. That's like calling a friend and asking, "You lived in Toledo once — does the airport ever get fogged in?" Or, as I was asked by a writer the other day, "Do you know anything about IQ testing?" And, eager to give my opinion as usual, I went on about my experience with the test, which was personal and not professional. That writer needs to talk to someone who both gives and reads the tests. Fiction authors are secondary sources; just because it's in one novel doesn't mean it's correct.

Another and more insidious cause of bad facts is invention and convenience. I asked a friend who wrote a techno-thriller why he had a helicopter refuel a jet at 50,000 feet when no chopper can fly at that altitude and his answer was, "Because I needed it to." That's working backward. I read a manuscript in which a cop walked into a bank, flashed his shield at the manager, and asked for the balance in someone's account, plus the depositor's home address. The author said a bank manager told her that's how it was done. This worried me; I didn't like to think personal information was that easily accessed and I didn't believe it. I knew, however, that the author needed the cop to get the information for the plot to proceed. I called a friend who is a cop — he told me that the above action was a direct violation of Fourth Amendment rights and no cop with a brain would attempt that.

Remember that when you're dealing with a genre audience, you're dealing with avid readers. It's unlikely that your techno-thriller will be your reader's first of that type. (And your own better not be the first one you've read!) Readers of police procedurals are very familiar with police procedure; readers of fantasy are familiar with magical concepts.

If a medical horror novel is to be credible, believable and entertaining, it should not only pass muster with readers of that genre, it would be ideal if the details impressed even a physician. How do you do that? Get a physician as a source—a physician of the type you need—not a dermatologist to brief you on autopsy procedure, but a pathologist who does them. In the above example about the bank, the author asked a banker to advise her on police procedure and that was the flaw.

There are situations in which a novelist asks a reader to suspend his disbelief, and the above case of the helicopter could have been constructed in such a way. If the author could reasonably develop a futuristic aircraft that can circle the earth at over 100,000 feet, why not develop its refueler as well? The reader already assumes these aircraft do not yet exist and the author has already made their technological possibility credible. Likewise, the cop—it is possible that a clever detective could seduce or trick information out of a bank manager, or hang around the bank till the depositor came in and then follow him, or a number of things.

In science fiction, fantasy and time-travel novels the reader is willing to suspend disbelief, provided the author makes the possibility credible with a few correct facts.

You can reasonably get hints from other fiction writers, but you can't count on them to give you the facts. If a favorite author claims a certain general was killed in the war of 1812 at a specific battle site, you must *still* take a trip to the library and reference this material. Believe me, your mail will reflect a certain amount of disbelief even if you check and cross-check everything.

A pause. You will note and intellectually argue that this is fiction and that many popular authors make similar and chronic mistakes. Everyone understands they're "making it up." And, they make money, too. My friend with the helicopter that can refuel at 50,000 feet is making more money than I am. If that argument holds any logic for you, we are not after the same things. This is not a book about making money. This is about writing quality genre fiction that works. Believe me, there is already plenty of competition for mediocre and bad books; the competition for well-written, finely tuned novels is much less. There are very few short cuts, very few things you can "fake."

In chapter nine, I'll speak at length about studying fiction. For the time being let me say one thing: It is perfectly appropriate for you to enjoy what you are reading when you study novels for structure and technique. But, if you are now a student of novel writing, you can no longer afford to indulge in the mindless pursuit of being completely entertained. You must now begin to take a closer look at why and how novels work. Or don't.

The Mechanics of Storytelling

Flow

For your plot, your plan of action, to move steadily from beginning to end, you must pay attention to a few technical details. Consider tense, transitions, voice and point of view as elements that keep your story moving at a good pace and make it easy for your reader to follow. These are the common storytelling devices that orient your reader to the who, what, when, where. Why will be discussed in chapter five.

Tense: Stories are traditionally told in the past tense. "I grew up slowly beside the marshes . . . " in lieu of, "I grow up slowly . . . " which is present tense. The most important thing to remember about tenses is to not mix them willy-nilly. It's the kiss of death to bounce from past tense to past perfect to present tense inside a single paragraph.

Present tense: He goes.

Past tense: He went.

Future: He will go.

Past perfect: He had gone.

Past participle: He has gone.

When the narrative calls for flashback information, the writer generally uses the past perfect tense, which is history and snaps the reader out of the action and tosses him backward into some recalled action. "He punched the police officer," versus, "He had punched the police officer." When flashback is called for, a transitional sentence that orients the reader to time and space is required.

I have seen a novelist shift gears into present tense occasionally and, when done well, the effect is both daring and dramatic. One must be very certain the reader can follow. Frances Donnelly used the present tense frequently in her novel *Shake Down the Stars*:

> Lucy visibly shrinks back from the venom in Virginia's tone. Virginia regards her dispassionately. "For God's sake, don't look so wounded, Lucy. As I said before, the Musgraves don't marry servants."
>
> By now there are two corresponding spots of color in Lucy's face.

Transitions: Sentences or paragraphs that bridge time, space and tenses. *Jamie had been watching television when her parents' argument escalated into a fistfight. She passed this information on to the police when they arrived.*

That mixture of tenses serves as a transition, bringing the reader to the present.

The new novelist who has trouble with transitions is usually laboring under the misconception that the reader needs every single detail of how the character's time is filled. The reader wants only the pertinent details and wants to get on with the story. Here are some examples of transitions:

"So, are we on for Sunday?" he asked.

Her answer was "yes" and not for just that Sunday, but for the next eight Sundays, and Saturdays, and Friday nights. By the end of two months he was finally confident enough to discuss his plans for the future.

Another:

Although she was terrified of the childbirth experience, she found there was no time for fear. Her labor started and the baby was born in less than four hours. Her joy was unsurpassed by any experience of her life, which probably explained why her second pregnancy followed so quickly. A year after her son's birth, she delivered her daughter, just as easily.

Those examples show big leaps in time, but a transition is effective for short jumps, too:

"I'm going to kill him," she said with conviction. But in the early hours of the morning when rage kept her from sleeping, she decided death was too good for him. The dark circles under her eyes the next day caused her to reconsider murder.

Transitions move time and people. Don't stay too long in one place and time. Your reader wants to see the next pertinent and significant event or action or behavior; keep your story and people moving and don't bother the reader with insignificant details. If what he's wearing doesn't have direct pertinence to the plot or character, don't dress him in the morning—let him show up in the next scene dressed casually or formally or don't mention it at all.

Voice: The big trauma to avoid in fiction writing is the passive voice. The passive voice removes the characters the furthest from the story action:

The ball was pitched by Tom. The TV was watched by Jamie. Passive. Tom and Jamie are being acted upon rather than acting. Characters who *act* are much more compelling than characters who don't. The alternative is the active: *Tom pitched the ball* or *Jamie watched television.* The active voice brings immediacy to the story whereas the passive drags the story down and often backwards.

Point of view: The vantage point from which the story is told. It is generally a good idea to stick with one point of view throughout the story. There is first person: "I grew up near the marshes. . . ." This is the only narrator allowed now. Everything the reader knows comes from the storyteller's perspective. That means other characters can be exposed only through their dialogue and visible actions; they cannot think or ponder, and the storyteller can't get into their heads. You have to rely on the narrator's impressions of other characters to characterize them.

There is third-person multiple point of view: "He grew up near the marshes and believed himself to be blessed. . . ." The perspective is his, the guy who grew up near the marshes, but can shift to the perspective of another person occasionally. There must be a clear transition so your reader knows you've changed to the point of view to another character, telling the story from a new vantage point. Once the arrow points to a character, that character's perspective is dominant. This subjective point of view allows the character to think and feel.

There is objective third person: "He grew up near the marshes, reaching six feet by his fourteenth year." This is still third person, as above, but the objective point of view sees the character through the camera—what he thinks and feels is not relevant to the storytelling. Only that which can be observed or heard is used.

And, there is omniscient observer: "They gathered near the marshes. Tom was the tallest and felt the most secure. Susan was the smallest and felt most vulnerable. The twins were in-between; solid in size but weak in courage."

That is the voice of a storyteller from above, like God, that gets into everyone's head and sees everyone's actions. It is difficult to keep the reader oriented in this voice. Sometimes the omniscient voice allows for moments of author intrusion, something Tom Robbins and Kurt Vonnegut are both known for. They have paused in the storytelling to discuss typewriters or breakfast cereal with the reader. You have to be pretty talented and cagey to get away with it. And the omniscient observer can get away with telling a story in present tense (all or partly) more easily than the other viewpoints.

The novelist chooses the point of view with several considerations:
1. Who is the most important character in the story?
2. How does the perspective of the storyteller relate to the plot needs?
3. Which point of view gives the greatest advantage?

In most stories the third-person multiple point of view is advantageous, giving the author the authority to spend the majority of time in the most important character's perspective, but looking at the perspectives of others when it serves the plot.

The first-person perspective is very limiting, but some plot lines are best served by this approach. I chose first person once to tell the story of a woman targeted by a psychopath. She knew the killer, but didn't know she knew him — he was a man close to her. I chose first person because I didn't want the reader to know who the psychopath was, and had I used a multiple point of view I would have withheld information from the reader by having an opportunity to be in a killer's head and not using it. I wanted the reader to come to the conclusion at the same time as the protagonist.

And omniscient observer can be effective whenever the story type benefits from the private thoughts of all the various characters — the observer can pop into everyone's thoughts at will. Though I will say again, the only thing that matters is that the reader always knows who is thinking and speaking or the entire effort fails.

The most common genre viewpoints are first person (only my thoughts and perspective), third-person subjective (one character's thoughts and perspective), and multiple third-person subjective (the thoughts and perspectives of more than one character, taking turns, with appropriate transitions). The omniscient observer (the thoughts and perspectives of all the players) is rarely used in genre because the writer often has one (or more) character(s) whose thoughts, if not deeds, are concealed to build tension, string out a mystery, surprise other characters, or for other reasons.

Tense, transitions, voice and point of view are, like using a dictionary and punctuating, purely technical storytelling devices. They're used in whatever way best serves the plot line and the characters' needs. These techniques, executed properly, are no substitute for good characterization or compelling plot lines. However, not using these techniques properly can severely damage an otherwise good story, just as misspellings and failure to punctuate will make an otherwise good story unreadable.

These technical devices can be easily found in the fiction you read. Ask yourself:

1. At what time did this happen and how did the writer establish that?

2. How did the writer move the story from then to now, from her to him, from now to then, from here to there?
3. Whose thoughts are these and how did the writer establish that?

Remember, use these techniques to keep the reader oriented to time, place, character perspective and to keep the story moving.

CHAPTER 5

Motivation:

"Why?"—The Story Glue

I t is not enough that she loves and wants him. It is not enough that she is beautiful, talented, intelligent and he is handsome, masterful and clever, and she loves and wants him. The reason heroine wants hero is the fulcrum on which the credibility of the romance balances.

Likewise, it is not enough that Bob is a murderer and John has to catch him because it's his job as a police detective. It is a reason without being reason enough for a good story. In a good suspense novel or mystery the protagonist is driven to find the clue or catch the criminal for reasons that are either deeply personal, intrinsic to his/her makeup, necessary for survival, or other compelling and believable reasons. The motivation is what gives the story forward thrust.

The *reason why* something happens or someone acts the way they do has everything to do with whether or not the novel works. This surpasses characterization because no amount of information on a person makes his/her actions automatic.

Take the example about character histories from chapter three—the girl who grew up deprived in a poor and dangerous neighborhood. To provide that history and go on to explain that she became a doctor does not explain enough. You might think the reader should follow the course, assume that impoverished conditions of childhood motivated the girl toward success. Since the same character history could precede a character locked in poverty all her life, you haven't led your reader as purposefully through the motivation as you need to for a strong and convincing story. This is a simple and easy-to-accomplish technique once you are aware of its function. "Because Sarah had always been both bright and determined, because she had seen misery and illness go unattended in her neighborhood and felt compelled to change that

atrocity, she worked against unbelievable odds to become a physician."
Because is the key. She is now motivated. The motivation is acceptable
because it is believable. It is believable because we have all heard of
this scenario—well-known cases of poor boy or girl makes good. Half
the successful people I've read about claim poor childhoods; the details
may change but the facts don't lie. This can be done—with the right
recipe.

That sounds awfully simple. It actually is. Sometimes the largest
roadblock comes from concentrating so hard on characterization and
plotting that you forget to keep yet another ball in the air—the motivation ball; everything happens for a reason. Here are some of the balls
the writer has to juggle (so far):

1. A character's basic traits enable him to do what he has to
   do, and a fundamental plot line gives the reader a specific
   something to hope for.
2. Additional complementary traits expand his character as he
   moves through events that create conflict and cause rising tension as the plot develops.
3. A history, certain values, and other conflicting characters while
   the story line builds intensity (probably adding one or a few
   subplots). The character's need grows proportionately to the
   necessity of reaching the story goal.

Now, you must add to those things two motivating factors:
1. Why he is the type of person who can do what has to be done.
2. Why what has to be done is important for that person to do.

Those two reasons combined will explain why there is a story. Why
is James Bond the best guy to undermine the bad guys before they
successfully take over the world? Because he has the skills and the
experience. And why should he do it? Because not only is he the best
suited, if he doesn't, the bad guys will take over the world.

The story goal is for the hero and heroine to fall in love. She is the
type to develop this relationship by winning his love because she is
desirable, tenacious and suited to him; it is important for her to do it
because she has loved and desired him since childhood, but her father
forced her to marry someone else. Now, as a young widow, her feelings
unchanged, she pursues her love.

Motivation must match and be supported by character traits and plot
requirements.

Credibility: The Reader's Trust

The Rule

The first step to creating good motivation for your characters and your plot is to become a student of basic psychology and human nature. Writers should know how people will usually behave, react and respond—what is *generally accepted* is something your reader understands and believes with a minimum of convincing. We know some obvious things—when one is cut, one bleeds. When one has not slept in two days, one is tired. How about "A mother will protect her child," and "A guard dog will bite an assailant." When story details become more complex, more complex motivation and an explanation of what is generally believed to be true is in order. The motivational reason why must be based on facts that are understood and details that are accurate.

Before going further, let's look at what happens when the general rule (fact and detail) is ignored in favor of a plot need. One of my students had a character who was the chief financial officer of a successful, publicly held corporation for over ten years. The fictional company was the tenth largest in the U.S. The plot called for a corporate overthrow of the officers; the character was a self-possessed, confident man who disliked being challenged by diverse opinions. I read the scene in which the angry character complained to his wife about his rage over the possibility of losing votes, losing his elevated position. So far everything is fine—character and plot are working well together. Then—whoops—the character begins to express his anxiety over being fifty years old and possibly jobless. The fear of joblessness as motivation was meant to cause the character's ensuing desperate acts to save his position.

Because my first question is "why is so successful a man nervous about joblessness?" there is a problem with the motivation. It doesn't match what I know about CFO's or corporate success—but the author needs the character's fear of joblessness. I get a picture of Lee Iacocca standing in the unemployment line. The story sags for me because I think the chief financial officer of a company of that size and success would probably have headhunters calling him with job offers, not to mention the fact that if he were any kind of a CFO he would have a provision for a high-priced severance. The writer, in this case, is clear on character traits that work and on a plot line that is believable—but he doesn't know what is typical behavior, typical reaction and response for a man in that particular set of circumstances.

Research helps immensely, but subjects like psychology, sociology, history and religion teach that people are driven (motivated) by their physical, intellectual, emotional and spiritual makeup as well as by cultural and historical data. It isn't necessary to be an expert on everything to write a good novel. What is necessary is to learn how people are known to behave in given situations. Successful novelists know how to research and become students of human nature.

If you're writing a novel about an adult woman who was physically abused as a child, learn about child abuse and its affects. If you're writing about a homicidal religious fanatic who thinks she has identified the Antichrist and must kill him, study the psychology of religious psychosis and fanaticism, as Koontz probably did. It isn't necessary to read volumes; you don't have to be ready to hang out your shingle and treat these people. The idea is to be convincing and that means either you have to research until you *know* the general facts or you have to guess right. In the long run, research is more time-effective and reliable. Just as you don't want to make up the facts and details when plotting, you don't want to guess at the proper motivation.

Knowing the generally accepted motivation is essential because it's the exception to accepted motivation that makes novels most interesting.

The Exception

In the example of the CFO about to be blackballed, if the writer knew basic facts about corporate politics and typical characteristics of a man in that position, he could build in the exception, making this an extraordinary situation with extraordinary motivation.

> Bill was terrified of joblessness at his age, a concern a clever CFO shouldn't have. He had sold his stock to finance his wife's spending addiction and had desperately accepted a contract with no severance condition because in a weak and panicked moment, he had embezzled from his company. His CEO had given him one more chance, his last. Then his boss died. Bill's reputation in the business world was worse than shaky. This company was the only thing he had left. Once ousted, no other corporation would take a chance on him.

Not only is Bill's reaction to the takeover now motivated, it is also more interesting than the predictable story. It's important to note that the exception that makes the story extraordinary only works when the writer knows and can explain the facts in the first place, provide a basis for comparison, and give a credible reason why this particular motivation is different. Koontz did this in *The Servants of Twilight*. Detectives, cops and even a noted psychiatrist went on record as stating that this was no ordinary religious fanatic — this was a special case, a very serious psychosis combined with a special kind of charisma that enabled her to control even more fanatics.

In all genres, the particular motivation is what makes the typical story special. It's a bit of contrast and comparison added to what your reader has come to expect. Characters can't just do things because of their traits, their personalities . . . and they can't just do things because the plot requires them to. Everyone thinks about what they will do; everyone weighs pros and cons to their actions. Even spontaneous actions are born out of values, strengths, weaknesses, predisposition. We all respond to events and situations differently and even when we don't spend a great deal of time deciding how to react, we can generally explain later what moved us to react in the way we did.

Motivation that is typical should remain in some balance with motivation that is unusual or extraordinary. This helps to show the contrast of characters through carefully planned contradictory actions. This refers to characterization—if your character is mostly strong, confident and determined, she will be motivated most of the time by her strength, confidence and determination. Then, when contrast is needed, the motivation is something extraordinary that undermines her basic traits. There are two ways to go at this:

1. Build a scene around a motivating factor.
2. Go into a scene and provide a motivation.

One of my favorite characters is Lilly. She is strong, confident, determined, intelligent and stubborn. She refuses to choose between work and true love because she believes it is possible to have both, even though the year is 1875. Lilly loves children and it appears that the only way she will raise a family is to sacrifice her dreams and beliefs and become a wife who is dominated by a man. She sees only bad options ahead—to give up work for family or to give up family for work; both unacceptable to Lilly. And I need Lilly to cry, to show the contrast in her character, to show the seriousness of her quest. She won't cry over little disappointments, she won't cry from a difficult challenge, and she isn't typically self-pitying. In my mind, one thing might cause Lilly to feel hopeless enough to weep: if she dearly wanted a child and thought she might never have one.

A scene that would force Lilly to face that disappointment is her selfish, lazy, self-indulgent sister's pregnancy. Patricia is not happy to be pregnant; she doesn't want to lose her figure and hates her husband, and by extension, her child. Lilly not only envies Patricia's pregnancy, but is also heartbroken at the thought of the birth of an unloved baby. Lilly has only loved once, that man lost to her. After the upsetting conversation with her sister, she sits alone in her darkened room and quietly cries. (How she cries is an important character consideration — this particular woman wouldn't stomp or rage; she would find the weakness of her tears somewhat embarrassing.) When her grandmother finds her (stunned by what she finds, for Lilly is the last person to indulge self-pity), Lilly has the opportunity to list her reasons for this behavior.

Hopefully, after that scene, my reader will wonder how or if Lilly will find a way to combine work and true love. As the motivation strengthens the scene and lends dimension to the characters, it also makes the need for the resolution a bit more desperate, puts more at stake.

The reverse of this is to have a plot requirement into which you must build the appropriate motivation. This example is from a manuscript I recently read: A young woman is being pursued by a dangerous hit man and is being protected by a private detective. They are about to escape from the small town they've been hiding in and the author needs one more obstacle, one more conflict so that their escape is not too easy. Although the hit man is watching the local bank, the only place he has thus far connected to the woman, and although the detective and the woman know that the bank is being watched, it is the bank where the paths of the woman and the hit man are most likely to cross. Anyplace else would be convenient, coincidental and therefore not clever enough. What the author needs in such a situation is a *reason* the woman *must* go to that bank despite the danger involved. What the author created for motivation was evidence against the hit man that the woman had placed in a safety deposit box. She *must* have that evidence — without it she can never prove the bad guys are bad and she would never be safe.

The evidence is one part of the motivation; the author still needed more. The detective and the woman can't act against their own instincts for survival by waltzing past the hit man into the bank. The author first showed their need to retrieve the evidence, then acknowledged their intelligence by having them devise a plan to get in and out of the bank without being seen by the hit man. Although the woman is fully disguised, there is a detail like her shoes or purse that the hit man recognizes. Now, finally, it is reasonable for the confrontation to occur.

The author had to motivate:
1. The trip to the bank.
2. The behavior of the woman and detective.
3. The hit man recognizing the woman despite her efforts to disguise herself.

Had the author just allowed the confrontation to happen without the appropriate motivations, the reader would have been mentally screaming, "Why go to the bank? Only a stupid person would sashay past the hit man!" With the motivation the reader is mentally asking, "Will they make it?" Which question causes disbelief and boredom and which question causes the tension and urgency to rise?

1. Motivation is the reason why a character acts the way he/she does, or the reason why a situation or event happens. In Lilly's case, she weeps because the thing she wants most in the world appears lost to her. This is prompted by her sister's pregnancy, which puts the issue close to home. In the case of the woman and detective, there is a dangerous confrontation brought on by the believable necessity for the woman to retrieve vital evidence from a safety deposit box.

2. Motivation stems from character traits but is never considered automatic; the motivation causes the behaviors or events. Though it is known that Lilly wants children, it is her strength in shouldering disappointments that would be expected—her sister's behavior *causes* Lilly's tears, a contrasting trait. The woman's need to get the evidence created the event of the confrontation with the hit man.

3. The basis for all motivation stems from what is *generally accepted* about a behavior or event; the exception to the rule is best explained through comparison to what is generally accepted. In Lilly's case, her tears are compared to her usual strength (her grandmother is shocked, she tries to hide her own tears out of embarrassment).

4. Motivation must follow facts and details that are correct; when the details are sketchy, the motivation is usually off and the story sags. Had the woman and detective gone to the bank for money, red flags would go up, for the reader knows about instant teller machines, wire services and just plain doing without the money if your life is at risk. There is only one way to get something out of a safety deposit box, while there are several ways to either get or do without money.

Motivation, naturally, runs through the entire novel. People are motivated and situations (events, conflicts) are motivated. People don't just do things without cause, and events don't just happen without a reason. Effective motivation leads the reader to a conclusion—to attempt to lead the reader to an assumption is the kiss of death in a story.

Pitfalls

Some of the most common failures in motivating characters or plots occur from the following:

1. Foolish and/or spontaneous actions. This is the woman who goes down into the cellar when she could have called the police. The action

or behavior becomes appropriate when the motivation is appropriate. Put the woman's child in the cellar, at risk, and she might not wait for the police to arrive.

2. Arbitrary decisions and/or behaviors. This is the character who needs vital information only her mother can provide, but accepts her mother's decision not to discuss the matter. This is the man who is in love with the woman who carries his child, plans to marry her and love her forever, but decides not to communicate with her in any way until his divorce is final. Obviously, making the behavior *purposeful* makes the motivation believable. Kill the mother off, making the vital information less accessible. Have the pregnant woman be unaware that her lover is getting a divorce and therefore go away to parts unknown to have her baby in privacy, making it impossible for him to contact her.

3. Actions prompted by passive needs or emotions. This is a subtle error that can loom large in story believability. A woman whose abusive husband believes she cannot swim, fakes her own drowning to escape him; she has secretly taken swimming lessons at the YMCA for a year and has become a strong swimmer. The critical plot twist in that scenario from *Sleeping With the Enemy* comes when an acquaintance from the Y calls the "deceased" woman's husband at his office to both introduce herself as a friend of his wife's and express condolences. It is this phone call that tips the husband off; he now suspects his wife is alive and the central conflict is his pursuit of her. There is a reason for the phone call plot-wise, but the phone call doesn't stem from a strong reason. The woman who phones had many other options—her need to call the husband was not serious but passive, which verges too close to coincidence. She could have sent a card, written a letter, or done nothing. She had nothing more to say to the husband than that she knew his wife and was sorry she had drowned. A bill to renew membership at the Y is not passive and would have caused the husband to investigate. Or, the woman who phoned could have had a pressing need, like an attempt to return some personal items left in the "deceased" woman's locker.

Phone calls out of the blue, going to the bank to get something that isn't badly needed when the bank is under surveillance by your enemy, or tears over the loss of something a character never expressed a desire for are all examples of actions prompted by passive needs or emotions.

Strong and convincing motivation should be relatively easy to accomplish once the writer is clear on the purpose. Every time someone in a story does something or behaves a certain way, the writer asks why.

Every time something happens in a story, the writer asks why. When the answer is a strong reason and that reason is in the manuscript, is correct in fact and detail, is convicted and convincing, is believable either because it is typical or is a logical exception to what is typical, the motivation is probably there.

CHAPTER 6

Dialogue:
Say What?

There are only two giant functions of dialogue in general:
1. Dialogue must characterize and individualize the speaker.
2. Dialogue must give the plot, the story, forward thrust.

Keeping these two functions in mind the novelist will eliminate nonessential chitchat, long-winded greetings and purposeless prattle. Also eliminated are all speeches that are contradictory to character or are generic in quality.

Let's look closely at the first function. This requires all the skills and techniques learned about characterization. You know the basic traits, the secondary traits, the contrasting traits. You understand what motivates your character. Listen to that character's voice in your head. He or she will probably sound like someone you've known or heard, perhaps a friend, a relative, an actor or a composite of several people. The voice you hear will contain all the strengths, weaknesses, dialects, verbal tics and personal values of that character.

Characterization should naturally include individualization of that person. There is no place more appropriate to show this than in dialogue. Your characters *sound* different from each other. This is the time to select appropriate and specialized speech patterns and habits. Only *one* character in your story uses the habitual endearment "hon." Only one person chronically uses snappy clichés in speech, like, "He'll be on me like a cheap suit," and "That should go over like a turd in a punch bowl." If you allow more than one character these specialized affectations, the characters become generic. It happens in life that many family members or groups of close friends use the same patterns, euphemisms, clichés, but in a novel the characters blur together when this happens.

It's like giving several characters the same first name.

The same name is a perfect example because it is so much like giving two characters the same voice. One of my students gave the two primary characters, father and son, the name Bob. There were no nicknames involved and no good reason other than the fact that it's a common occurrence. It became difficult for the reader to recognize and separate them when they were both present in a scene and took too long to identify which Bob when one was alone in a scene. When it comes to dialogue, there should be enough individualization to what characters will say and how they will say it so that the tag, "Bob said" should not be necessary every time.

Perhaps people who are closely related share common usages, tics and habits. In the novel we have the option of showing distinctive individual traits and contrasts by assigning characters dialogue that is unique to that person, just as we choose names that are unique and different.

What the characters say is as individual as how they speak. Ideally the characters have obvious differences not just in the way they say things and their individual verbal preferences and habits, but in *what* they say according to their personalities, traits, values and goals.

Look at three women with an identical problem. They each have a son in a high school biology class in which the teacher is a tyrant. The students have the same trouble in understanding what's expected of them, finishing projects, and getting decent grades because the stress level is so high due to the teacher's screaming and abuse. The first woman is shy and reserved and dislikes conflict. The second is a teacher herself, self-confident in this situation, and very fair-minded. The third is caustic, combative and likely to develop a conflict if there isn't one handy to take on. Which of the following statements comes from which mother?

"Listen, you jerk: I will *not* have my son abused in your class-room, and if you retaliate for this phone call in any way, we will be at war. And I *like* war!"

"I wonder if we might sit down together—you, Tommy and I—and discuss this communication problem? I know Tommy only wants to clear things up and get the instructions straight so he can do well in your class. He's having such a hard time."

"Unfortunately, what I'm hearing from parents of students in your classes is that the communication problem is exacerbated by your screaming and yelling. This worries me and I consider it serious. We can either sit down to discuss this together, or we can sit down with the principal, but the problem needs to be resolved right away."

You can surely tell which is which. Different personalities handle identical problems in various ways. While this should seem obvious, it isn't. Even the skilled novelist sinks into the trap of thinking people should sound as they sound in life. Sometimes the characters all say what the novelist would have said. Novels are meant to reflect life, enlarge life, mirror life, satirize life, and more. Just as with characterization, in which the human contradictions could only confuse the reader, in dialogue characters have more differences in their words than ordinary people.

On my fourteenth novel, the editor complained that my characters sometimes sounded alike. And, he added, "Don't tell me that you and your husband share the same verbal tics, buzz words and euphemisms because I don't want to read about you and your husband." On closer inspection I noticed that three different characters resorted to identical profanity under the same circumstances; all three had used the common verbal cliché, "He'll be on me like a cheap suit." Perhaps it is realistic that three different personalities would all say, "Dammit!" when a plate broke, a bra strap broke, or a tire went flat. In real life. However, in the novel these three characters with similar dialogue were:

- An articulate, well-educated, poised, confident female lawyer with a successful career in law for over ten years.
- A loose and goosey, humorous but skilled Los Angeles police detective who takes risks and enjoys giving provocative statements and quips.
- A sociopath who cleverly manipulates and masquerades as the citizen of the year by appearing to be a most helpful and sensitive man.

These characters are about as diametrically opposed as could be, a thing I did purposely. They bounced off each other superbly; they all came from different backgrounds, had different values, different goals, opposing traits. Developing characters that diverse (particularly in a suspense novel) helps elevate the tension, sustain unpredictability and entertain. It's the kiss of death to then allow them generic, all-purpose dialogue. The cure (once I saw the problem clearly), was to examine this more closely and make some choices. I decided the cop would be liberal and humorous with profanity, the lawyer would use it rarely and only for impact and even then in an intelligent manner, and the killer would be humorless, avoid habitual and spontaneous speech patterns, and be as pragmatic in choosing his words as he was in choosing his victims and evading police. Which of the characters described above said which thing in a highly charged, emotional situation?

"Wonder what law he broke? Harassment? Illegal disposal of body parts? Too bad there isn't a law against being psycho. This guy is gonzo."

"Well, I get it! I damn *sure* get it — he's playing with my mind! It was him all along . . . just think about it!"

"You said you weren't going to let me move in and take care of you, which I seemed all too willing to do. Well, I'm not that damned willing. I was trying to be thoughtful."

Words With Feeling

Dialogue is a perfect place to deliver the individual emotional impact of the characters — how people feel inside. Objective narrative only begins the process. What they say, how they respond to what is said *to* them, and their chosen replies *prove* the emotion that has been promised. If your character is described as outspoken, feisty and fair-minded, she will initiate dialogue and respond in dialogue in ways that are outspoken, feisty and fair-minded.

As an example, let's take the mother who is a teacher, confident, fair-minded and neither passive nor combative, and put her in a conversation with the tyrannical biology teacher. (I chose her specifically; passive characters seldom charge up dialogue and highly combative characters sometimes come off as caricatures. This is close, yet not too close, to real life.) Look at how the narrative description of what she is doing and feeling plays into dialogue that substantiates the claim. I've italicized character description that relates to emotion and emotional reaction:

Dotty Harris had left four messages with the high school receptionist and still Mr. Johnson hadn't returned her call. Tommy was becoming more and more distraught over his failing Biology grade and admitted he feared the teacher. *Fear was not an emotion Dotty was feeling. She would not leave another message. She would drive to the school. Having been a teacher herself, she found this failure to respond deplorable.*

The phone rang, saving her the trouble of a drive. She answered.

"Mrs. Harris, please," a deep and impatient male voice commanded.

"This is Mrs. Harris," she replied.

"Ben Johnson, returning your call."

"Thank you, Mr. Johnson. My son, Tommy is having difficulty in your class and I thought we should talk about it."

"What hour?"

"What hour?" Dotty replied, *confused*.

"What hour is his class?" he repeated.

My God, he doesn't even *know* who my son is, she thought. "Fourth hour, Mr. Johnson," she said, just as curtly. "Do you have more than one Tommy Harris?"

"Fourth hour. Okay. What's the trouble?"

"A near-failing grade is the trouble. And added to that, Tommy tells me he doesn't understand what assignments are due, when they're due, and what you expect of him."

"He should pay attention in class."

"He tells me he's doing his best and that his efforts are complicated by tirades during which you scream and swear at the students."

"Oh? Well, Mrs. Harris, tell you what: I won't believe everything the kids say about the parents if you don't believe everything the students say about the teachers. Hmmm?"

"Other parents I've contacted have heard similar complaints. I won't have my son abused in your class. This has to be resolved."

"Mrs. Harris, since there are no bruises, this is wasting my time. Just tell Tom to pay attention in class, do his work, study for his tests, and we'll get along just fine."

Dotty felt her cheeks grow warm. "Yes, Mr. Johnson, I will certainly do that. And I will also make an appointment with the principal to discuss this further, since you and I aren't getting anywhere. I'd like you to be included in that meeting, but it isn't necessary. I'll be bringing other parents whose children feel abused in your classroom and perhaps we'll find a way to communicate our needs. With or without your cooperation."

"Are you threatening me?"

Dotty laughed unpleasantly. "Well, perhaps that did sound threatening. Let me clarify what I mean. I was a high school teacher for twelve years and I'm very informed on classroom procedure, which of course does not include screaming and cursing. So, I'm more than willing to go the principal, and the president and the superintendent. I'm willing to go through the system until I believe my son is being treated with decency in your classroom and if you find that threatening, we have a bigger problem than I thought."

First, note how the description of her feelings and behaviors and attitudes feed into her tone of voice, her clipped and precise sentences or her longer, more eloquent ones. She is *not* afraid and she is clearly annoyed that the teacher hadn't called her sooner. Next, she is unsure what attitude she is dealing with, since the teacher asks what hour her son's class is. When she realizes the teacher can't even place her child, she becomes angry, unpleasant and tougher. What she chooses to say is supportive of those feelings.

Next, notice the dialogue setup. You would have a different feeling about Mr. Johnson had he said, "Is Mrs. Harris there, please?" rather than the clipped, "Mrs. Harris, please." Note that no time was wasted on small talk; Mrs. Harris did not have to say hello when she answered the phone as the reader can follow just as well assuming that "she answered" would include the greeting. Alternately, notice the emotional impact of repetitiveness; "What hour?" "What *hour*?", etc. Mr. Johnson is not a generous communicator; he is not cooperative or forthcoming. And, Mrs. Harris needs a moment to accept and cope with the blatant lack of cooperation from the teacher who didn't even know the student he'd been screaming and swearing at.

And especially note that this kind of conversation would be rare. Of course it could happen, but I've been raising kids for seventeen years and have talked to quite a few teachers. Even though I'm aggressive, I've never been quite that confrontational nor have I encountered a teacher (even the meanest ones with the worst reputations) who would speak that coldly and rudely to me. Dialogue is meant to be entertaining—it's meant to take risks, be provocative, show conflict, and stir up the emotions of the reader.

Moving Plot

Dialogue can allow characters to resolve their difficulties, but since your plot goal is to create obstacles, it is an even better tool to show conflict. To that end, let 'em at each other! Give your characters the snappy comebacks that you, fuming at a recalled conversation, wish you'd thought of at the time. Now you have the time. Dialogue is the place to take the chances we avoid in everyday life—it's time to be sassy, confrontational, brutally honest, convicted, risky. Consider this scenario: A woman who struggles with an extra twenty pounds has worn her best dark-colored cocktail dress to a party. It's slimming and flattering. But her archrival, a slim, fair woman, managed to turn a compliment into a cruel dig. "Why, Mary, what a chic dress, and how thin it makes you look. Dark purple is just the thing to hide those few figure embellishments, isn't it, dear? I'm afraid that color would almost make me look *too* slim." In real life, at least in my experience, Mary would be struck speechless and would go home either hurt, depressed, enraged or something. Speechless characters, however, are not useful. The novelist would take that situation and make it more fun. More tense, more conflicted and more exciting. The novelist might allow Mary to stand straight, show a slight and superior smile, and say, "I don't know about making you look too slim, Priscilla, but I doubt this shade of purple would do much for that unique color you use on your hair. What's it called?"

Sound mean and biting? Good, I hope so. I've been to a lot of office parties in my day and they're rarely that much fun. We spend much of our lives attempting to be appropriate and polite; socialized people spend more time trying to defuse combative situations than trying to ignite them. In novels, however, readers want to see and hear things that are more provocative than the usual chitchat and small talk.

Dialogue is the perfect place for statements that have a pivotal effect on the plot, always more meaningful when a character reveals something significant than when the narrator shares something. Consider the following snatches of dialogue and how they might affect the story and the other characters.

"I was telling the truth when I said I love you, that I will never love a woman as I love you. I was also telling the truth when I said I couldn't marry you. I'm a Catholic priest."

"I'd love to tell you about your husband's death, about his last words and his desire that you know how much he loved you. But I don't think you want to hear it from me. I'm the one who killed him."

"I would give more of myself if I could. I want to, but do you really want me? Forever, you said. No matter what, you said. Could you still say that knowing I'm a vampire?"

Imagine how a plot moves when a character makes a discovery.

"He's my son, isn't he?"

"You weren't with your friends at the convention, were you, Dorothy? You were with *my* friend. My best friend. And you slept with him."

Discoveries, challenges, confrontations and startling secrets that show up in dialogue can set up a whole chain reaction of exciting movement. When the characters speak there is an immediacy for the reader. When something urgent is passed off in narrative, it can certainly cause action and move plot, but your reader still wants to hear what they say to each other. Consider: "It was that morning at the hospital that she became convinced that despite his devoted love, he wouldn't marry her.

She overheard the priest administering last rites to a patient, and it was his voice."

Definitely a pivotal spot, but your reader still aches to know what he will say when confronted. Or, how she will confront him. Dialogue is supposed to do for plot what steak sauce is supposed to do for steak—make a good piece of meat better. In deciding whether to drop that bomb in narrative or dialogue, simply consider the impact. The writer can often drop the bomb twice:

> She heard the priest administer last rites and recognized the voice of her lover. Stunned, she leaned against the wall outside the patient's room and listened. She wondered when her rage would subside enough to allow the pain of betrayal to crush her. How *could* he?

> That night, when he came to her, she did not embrace him as usual. Instead she smiled at him, though tears gathered in her eyes. "How was your day . . . Father Mike?"

Genre-Specific Dialogue

There are some obvious considerations in choosing the dialogue to match the genre you're writing in. Then again, there are some subtle considerations.

First, even the most inexperienced novelist knows better than to allow a 1990s CIA agent from Washington, D.C. to say, "Forsooth, Father Demetrius arrives anon!" Old West cowpokes have twangs, Southerners have drawls, foreigners have accents specific to their countries. Also, action-oriented plots don't contain many long-running, drawn-out conversations—it slows down the fast pace of the action and shorter dialogues, clipped sentences and fast volleys keep up that pace, even when there's enough of a lull in the action to warrant conversation. Conversely, the characters in a romance between two nobly bred English characters might be more on the well-articulated, longer sentence side, provided the tension of conflict is still present.

I've noticed that mystery novels tend to spend more time developing clues in dialogue than suspense novels do. In mystery, questions have to be answered; in suspense, someone has to escape danger. Where the pace of action is fastest, the type of dialogue tends to be more clipped; where the action is modulated and steady, the dialogue is likewise. Also, the amount of dialogue versus narrative description differs; the reader can almost tell from how it lays up on the page whether or not the writer is in a hurry. It is therefore the type of novel you're writing that commands the type of dialogue the characters indulge.

Two prime examples that come to mind are *Presumed Innocent* (a murder mystery) and *The Firm* (a suspense). In the first, the murder is over and while there is the worry that the wrong person could be convicted, we don't fear that anyone is in imminent danger. The way conversation ensues (most of the time) is less urgent:

"Listen," he says, "I gotta tell you something about your technique as an interrogator, Rusty. You beat around the bush too much. You have to learn to be direct."

We laugh, but I say nothing. If he wants off the hook, he'll have to wriggle.

"Let's say the decedent and I were both single and both adults," he finally says, looking down into his cup. "That isn't any kind of problem, is it?"

"Not if it doesn't give you any better idea who killed her."

"No," he says, "it wasn't that kind of thing. Who knew that dame's secrets? Frankly, it was short and sweet between us. It's been history, I'd say, four months."

That is the only dialogue on that page, the rest narrative. The investigation proceeds and while there is an urgency to find out who did kill her, there is no imminent danger, as the type of "talk" seems to signify.

Conversely, in *The Firm*, the protagonist is in danger from the beginning. He is virtually scrambling to escape danger throughout the novel and the dialogue is characterized by short, urgent volleys:

"You don't think they'll find us?"

"No way. No one followed you out of Memphis, and we detected nothing in Nashville. You're clean as a whistle."

"Pardon my concern, but after that fiasco in the bookstore, I know you boys are not above stupidity."

"It was a mistake, all right. We—"

"A big mistake. One that could get me on the hit list."

What is said and how it's said, characterized by cut-off sentences, interruptions and the like, give the impression of urgency. Also, that is a snatch of an entire page of fast-paced dialogue and very little narrative.

A more subtle aspect of genre-specific dialogue is the character's personal style in that character's specific setting. For example, the hero, speaking of his love for a woman, might say, "You're all that much more beautiful because you don't know how beautiful, how desirable you are." Or, a man of another style, in a different setting or genre might say, "Come here, baby. Love me." Still another guy says, "If you give me a chance, Susanna, I reckon I can make you love me."

Then, just as with characterization, motivation and plotting, the author has a golden opportunity to do the unexpected with stylized, genre-specific dialogue. That is the New Mexico sheriff in cowboy boots working on a case with tough, street-smart New York City cops. That is the British detective trying to solve a mystery in Texas.

Of course, as with every other aspect of the novel, the fiction writer must research dialogue. Once the writer knows what a person in that position/setting/socioeconomic level/etc. might say and how he might say it, then the writer can either opt for the general rule or create the exception. "Though born and raised in Texas, she had practiced her eastern U.S. dialect for years and there was no hint of the Yellow Rose in her voice."

The best research is usually talking to people (or hearing them speak through movies and television), but reading in the genre will prove helpful as well.

Pitfalls

Before moving on to practice methods for creating good dialogue, I'd like to talk about some of the hang-ups and pitfalls that prevent otherwise good writers from creating effective, high-quality dialogue.

First, although dialogue sounds like people speaking, it is not the same as real people in conversation. If you've ever listened to a tape of a conversation and understood it, but read the same unedited conversation in transcript, you know what I mean. It isn't the same as reading a movie script and then hearing it read; the movie script only lacks the inflection while the spoken words match those on the page. I recently watched a hidden camera newsreel videotape of legislators apparently taking bribes. The daily newspaper ran identical transcripts of the same event. The audio conversation was understandable though it was filled with run-on sentences, pauses, repetitions, diversions from the point, "ummms," "ahhhs" and "you-knows." The written dialogue was so disjointed it was difficult to follow.

In written dialogue, the writer must take control and direct the conversation. Dialogue in the novel is more crisp, clear and clean than real-life conversation.

Another difference from real-life conversation is that you have all the time in the world to think of what to say next. That is not so when you're confronted by the traffic cop who's writing out your speeding ticket. When your character is getting the ticket, you can take hours (or days or weeks) to decide what he's going to say. You can even go back and unsay what he said and resay it.

This is good news to the novelist who has trouble with dialogue. Even if you're shy and not given to quick comebacks, you have this advantage. You're not really on the spot. Dialogue is just more writing. Even though it has quotes around it, if you can come up with creative ways to describe a character or a setting, you can come up with a clever verbal exchange.

Another dialogue hang-up is embarrassment or intimidation. I encountered this on my first novel. In fact, it took me so long to figure out what was wrong, I became very discouraged. I have an advantage when it comes to creating dialogue; I happen to be a pretty good conversationalist and enjoy debate. I like (and make use of) quick comebacks and one-liners. However, the dialogue in my first novel was so achingly bad, I could hardly stand to reread it. It was also very hard to write in the first place.

I found that certain things people would say, particularly in situations rife with conflict or passion, embarrassed me. This clogged me up. When it came to any dialogue that would put zing in a story, words that would heighten passion or produce rage or terror, I simply couldn't think of anything. I felt *the burden of being appropriate*; the weight of saying the right thing as opposed to the interesting, provocative thing. Writing dialogue was, for me, like having my mother watch me make love.

The cure for me was simple — it was contained in a little psychological trick. "If I'm ever able to publish this novel, I will use a pseudonym and no one will ever know it was me who said that." My self-consciousness was gone. I put quotes around any sassy, seductive, provocative, ingratiating, threatening thing that popped into my mind. I eventually created a good book and when a publisher made me an offer, my plan to hide my identity was also gone.

This idea that *you* are saying (or have said or would say) these things has to go first. Having your protagonist tell off her mother-in-law is not you telling off yours. This syndrome is not only harmful to good dialogue, it can work hell on a plot. You can't write freely and creatively when filled with self-conscious inhibitions; self-conscious writers create stories that are too neat and tidy (read: dull).

Ego takes a hike during the creative process and the story becomes the focal point; people say and do what they must to make a compelling story. If you have too much ego involvement while writing you might be spending too much time wondering what effect this story is going to have on *you*. The side effects of that range from unrealistic and grandiose delusions to self-consciousness and embarrassment.

Along the same lines, I had another problem closely associated with the first. I found myself protecting my characters from each other as if protecting my child from a harsh word or action. I ended up with characters who couldn't be rude, courageous, passionate, honest or provocative. I took such good care of them, in fact, that the hero and heroine of my very first romance, despite the incredible problems of being from different social classes, distrusting each other, and having entirely different values managed to patch up their differences and fall helplessly in love. By page thirty.

The new writer can check herself against this kind of personal intimidation by simply asking a question: A friend of mine calls it "The Aunt Martha Syndrome." Whenever it crosses her mind that "Aunt Martha will die when she reads this," my friend knows she's on the right track with her idea or dialogue. She then types it up and worries about what Aunt Martha will say later. (The Aunt Marthas of the world are all alive and kicking.)

Practice

How do you get from here to there; from the desire to create good dialogue to actually doing it? One way is to isolate a provocative snippet or two and construct the rest of the conversation around it. Mitchell *might* have come up with, "My dear, I don't give a damn," as a final, crushing, irrevocable response for Rhett before she developed the four pages of dialogue that got her there. That final statement can work as a goal. Or perhaps she thought the dialogue: "Take my handkerchief, Scarlett. Never, at any crisis of your life have I known you to have a handkerchief," was perfect for Rhett to say in response to Scarlett's tears long before she developed the reason Scarlett was weeping or the scene in which it would occur.

Writers often develop drop-dead lines and exchanges that move the plot or characterize and then take the time necessary to get the verbal battle to that pitch.

"You shore are pretty when you're mad."

"Then I'm about to get a whole lot prettier."

If you think of a perfect piece of dialogue or exchange—make the most of it. Don't bury it in a long conversation but rather use it as a launching pad for a stunning verbal exchange. Or, end a scene or chapter with it so it can really stand out.

Not every piece of dialogue that's moving or touching or scorching is some unique combination of words never seen before. It isn't always like an original joke, new song or first-ever color combination. When dialogue works in concert with the character and the plot, simple and subtle statements can bring mountains crashing down.

I'm reminded of Tom Wingo in *The Prince of Tides*. He had been secretly teaching the son of a concert violinist to play football. The boy's father had forbidden sports because of the boy's hands and his future as a gifted musician. The mother had given in to the boy's incredible desire to play football by asking Tom to coach him without his father's knowledge. The boy had worked hard and was beginning to feel encouraged—he might actually make the team, when his father found out and not only forbade any further lessons, he promised to pack his son off to music camp for the summer. Tom Wingo told the man that in forbidding his son's football, he might make it all that much more desirable. Worse, in trying to force his son to be something he didn't want to be, he might lose him altogether.

"I'm his father and I assure you, he will be the violinist I've intended him to be," he said as he turned and walked toward his apartment building.

"I'm his coach," Tom said to his back. "And you have just created a football player, sir."

It's a very ordinary piece of dialogue, but the impact of it really struck me. It's subtle and effective. It changes the course of lives, of the story. Dialogue's job is not only to individualize, move the plot and intensify the story, but also to tell that character's truth—simply, cleanly, effectively and with conviction. When you think of a line or exchange that has that ring of clarity to it, construct a scene around it.

Practice using that same conviction in dialogue setups; it can be the thing that gets you going. You can set up the dialogue and pull the trigger on it without an extensive (and sometimes dull) lead-in of greetings, salutations and descriptions of where they are, how they got there, what they're wearing and how this scene began. The following is a little something about sisters, Beverly and her younger sister, Terry:

Terry was pretty, independent and sensible. Beverly actually admired her. Terry was also on the pill. You know, The Pill. Which was better than sleeping with Steve and not being on the pill. But Terry was barely twenty and couldn't possibly know what she was doing.

"Did," Terry corrected.

"Well, it's not too late," Beverly said.

"Yes it is, and you know it."

If you think you know what is *eventually* going to be said, you can practice using the immediacy of dialogue by opening chapters or scenes with it and doing a little flashback, if necessary, to fill the reader in on the action already taking place. Or, perhaps the facts of the scene were laid out in the end of the previous chapter. The one thing to watch with flashback and foreshadowing is the amount. It tends to keep the reader out of the action to remember everything or predict everything. This chapter opening comes from *Lonesome Dove*, and the end of the preceding chapter marked the somewhat emotional decision of the cowboys' long-time cook, Bolivar, to quit and go back to his family in Mexico:

"Well, if we wasn't doomed to begin with, we're doomed now," Augustus said, watching Bolivar ride away. He enjoyed every opportunity for pronouncing doom, and the loss of a cook was a good one. "I expect we'll poison ourselves before we get much farther, with no regular cook," he said. "I just hope Jasper gets poisoned first."

"I never liked that old man's cooking anyway," Jasper said.

"You'll remember it fondly, once you're poisoned," Augustus said.

If you've ever had the experience of finding a novel so engrossing that you're skipping long narrative passages and leaping to the dialogue to see what's going on with the people, then you know the obvious advantages of beginning a chapter with a good, effective exchange. It puts the reader instantly into the scene and provides the story with an immediacy that promotes page-turning.

There are other ways to practice writing good dialogue, and practice is the word. If you can learn to write at all, you can write effective dialogue also. It's a question of learning what's good, why it's good and how it worked. You can type up fictitious exchanges of fights, love scenes, confessions and the chatter that follows a funeral. Often, somewhere in that practice exercise you'll find something you can use in the novel.

Another practice method that I used in the beginning was to tape movies on an audiocassette. Not just any movie, mind you, but one in which you admire the dialogue and have a sense of why it works—because it's provocative, tense, exciting, whatever. (If you were to try this practice on *Poltergeist III* you would hear about an hour and a half of "Carrie Ann! Carrie Ann!" Pick a movie in which there is some snappy dialogue happening.) Now, take that tape to your typewriter or word processor and using the start and stop button on the tape recorder, type it up. Recall the scene and intersperse your dialogue with setting and characterization narrative as you see fit. Describe the speakers as you recall them. If you hear:

"There's nothing you can do, John. I'm leaving. I'm through."

"You think so, Marcia? You'd better think again."

"There's nothing you can do to stop me now. Steve is waiting in the car out front."

"Then you're not really through . . . you've just changed partners."

Okay, that's what you *heard*. Dialogue alone isn't going to make a book, but good dialogue trussed up by characterization, setting and plot thrust is going to make a book good. Now, in addition to their talk, add what you remember from the scene, or re-create your own scene so it reads like a novel:

She snapped the lock on her small suitcase and picked it up, turning to face her husband. Although color stained her cheeks, she lifted her chin bravely and stared at him levelly. "There's nothing you can do, John. I'm leaving. I'm through."

His lip curled meanly and he slowly looked her over, his dark eyes moving from her toes to the top of her head. "You think so, Marcia? Then you'd better think again."

"There's nothing you can do to stop me now," she said with conviction, although inside she was trembling. Would he hit her? Would he follow her? "Steve is waiting for me in the car outside," she informed him, hoping to forestall any violence against her.

John smiled cruelly. "Then you're not really through. You're just changing partners."

The above exercise helps the practicing writer to see how dialogue is useful, how it looks and feels in addition to how it sounds. It helps the writer to learn how to choreograph the dance steps of give-and-take, conversation, the tug-of-war of tension or passion between characters who are at odds. And remember that characters who are *not* at odds, who have no tension between them, whether it's the tension of love or hate, rarely do more in dialogue than exchange information. While that will be necessary from time to time, too much of that and too little of the other tends to make a good cracker soggy.

Another practice method is to rewrite the dialogue of another novelist. Take any scene and verbal exchange you like and revise it, sprucing it up, changing the point or the counterpoint. Or, take a long narrative piece describing a character or scene, and write it in dialogue as it's happening.

Everyone at some point has tried to prepare themselves to respond to something someone will say, which is next to impossible, but we still do it.

"I'm going to ask him for a $20,000-a-year raise."

"And if he says he can't justify it?"

"I'll point out that I sold twice that amount in insurance in just six months last year; would he rather not have the sales and pay an inferior salesman less?"

"What about commission? That will come up."

"I'm willing to compromise, reduce commission. I feel I need the salary to justify the work I do and verify the faith the company has in my ability."

Et cetera.

Write, without the need to stuff that writing into the novel, every fight, every subtle and sneaky manipulation, every wild lie, every seduction you can think of. Then add a twist and get yourself out of it, one way or another. See that example above? The next piece of dialogue could read: "And what if he brings up the fact that you stand on faithless ground since the suspicion that you've embezzled?"

Aha! Get out of that one, writer. Okay: "I don't think he'll do that. I have pictures of him naked."

See, writer . . . we're having fun because we're daring. And that's what dialogue is meant to be. Let the reader hear what people are saying to each other in boardrooms and bedrooms, while standing over a dead body or seducing a sexy librarian, while planning an assault or a prison escape. Dialogue is more fun than anything else because if you'll hang onto that combination of loose and brave, the people in your stories will say things to each other that will drive the reader wild with delight.

The most important advice I can give the writer who wants to create good dialogue is this: Let 'em at each other.

CHAPTER 7
Pacing:
The Unputdownable Novel

For me, there is no feeling in the world like being lost in a novel. There is no greater, more luxurious frustration than dying to get back to it, having my vision begin to blur from a need for sleep while the drive to finish the story burns as much as my eyes. A good, unputdownable novel. There's a pace, a rhythm, an urgency to complete the story, get to the end, yet a desire to savor every word. After years of reading, writing, criticism and study, it's harder for me to find those undeniably great stories. Of course there's no specific type of book that's the best book; this isn't about types. The best book in the world is the last one you loved to death and couldn't put down — never mind the reviews or numbers sold. When I find that book that absorbs my interest to the peak, it's an incomparable joy.

In the great novel the plot is compelling, the characters are vivid and memorable, and I'm filled with a sense of being in a different place and time because the setting is brought to life. That's pacing. That's balance and integration of the three major story components.

In a good novel three things happen to the reader to cause the rising desire to turn the page. The reader experiences a strong sense of place, whether it's a train in Pakistan or a laundry in Biloxi. Simultaneously, the reader develops a personal relationship with the characters that is built by the reader's ability to empathize, understand and believe them to be like real people. Because of this relationship and feeling of being transported into another place and time, the reader assumes their dilemma and thus, their need to resolve the problem, reach the goal, arrive with them at their conclusion.

Integration

Causing the three major story elements to work together, in balance, only requires being attentive to the technique. There is nothing different about the plot, characterization or description — just a different balance of information. Following are three technical jobs — a description of a setting, a description of a character, a description of a plot device or piece of action. First, look at how they're handled singularly. Following will be an example of the same information blended into a story scene.

1. The dining room seemed to sparkle with a life of its own. Wedgewood china, shocking white and rimmed with gold trim, and Waterford wine glasses and tumblers were cut in a pattern identical to two large candelabras that held six white candles each. The flatware was gold, possibly real. Fine Irish linen covered a dark mahogany table that could seat twenty and a fresh flower arrangement nearly three feet at its longest lay like a runner down the table. The wealth in this single room was more than many people earned in a year.

2. Shannon Lewis had worked against unbelievable odds to obtain her master's degree in sociology by her twenty-fifth year. She came from a family of slim means and modest education, though they were loving and devoted to her. Shannon had been blessed with a sharp mind and good looks; part-time modeling helped her earn the tuition money that was not covered by her academic scholarship. Now, at the age of twenty-seven she was a department head for a government social services agency, a woman of middle income, independent means, attractive and in love with Eric Wellington, a very wealthy young man.

3. Shannon Lewis is meeting Eric Wellington's family for the first time. His mother and two sisters have a formal dinner for her at the family home and Shannon is a nervous wreck. Though Eric tells her she looks fabulous, she feels inferior to the Wellington social status and their incredible wealth. Shannon hadn't eaten off china until she graduated from college! She could barely swallow her meal, and when Mrs. Wellington asked her a simple question she reacted with such panic that she dropped her wine glass and it spilled all over the white tablecloth. While trying to mop up her mess, she pushed back her chair too quickly and it fell over. She nearly fell over the chair and heard one of Eric's sisters laugh while the other gasped. Eric's mother's expression turned sour and grim. Shannon was doomed; they found her ridiculously inept.

Look at what happens to these three facets of the story when there's a bit of integration; when setting, plot and characterization work together in the telling.

Sheer nerves caused the fiasco that disrupted the Wellington dinner party. Shannon Lewis was having dinner with her fiancé's mother and two sisters for the very first time and their acceptance of her was all she craved. Eric told her repeatedly that it didn't matter that her family had been poor; it didn't matter that she didn't move in the same social circles.

She knew it didn't matter to Eric. She was afraid it might matter to the Wellington women.

"What does your father do, dear?" Mrs. Wellington asked.

She swallowed carefully, calmly, before answering. "He's an auto mechanic, Mrs. Wellington. He specializes in transmissions."

"In what, dear?"

That's when it happened. She meant to calmly lift her wine glass, an ancient and expensive Waterford cut, before elaborating, but she dropped the glass right on the china plate. Crystal and china broke. Naturally. A 1945 vintage Cabernet that cost more than Shannon's dress bled over an antique, Irish linen tablecloth, damping a virgin mahogany table. She heard a gasp from one of the sisters. Shannon leapt to her feet to try to contain the spill with her napkin, damaging more expensive linen, and knocked over her chair. She heard the other sister chuckle as the wine stain spread under an elaborate floral arrangement and bled on toward the crystal candelabra.

"Let it be, dear," Mrs. Wellington advised, her expression grim and sober. "We'll just have Matthews change the setting. Please."

Shannon straightened, nearly falling backwards over the toppled chair. Had Eric's arm not intercepted her, she might have been upside down on the floor with her skirt over her head.

Eric righted Shannon's chair for her. She checked expressions as she took her seat. She was doomed. After all the years of working against unbelievable odds to get an education—a master's degree in sociology—she couldn't manage a simple conversation with rich people. After all the modeling she'd done to pay for tuition her parents couldn't afford and her academic scholarship wouldn't cover, her natural grace had failed her and she'd been a total klutz. She had single-handedly turned a luxurious dining room that seemed to glitter with its own life into a shambles. The sale of her entire wardrobe couldn't set a table like this. And the Wellington women seemed to know it.

That short scene should illustrate how the writer can achieve a sense of time and place, a sense of character, and a plot action that is moving. I want my reader to get a sense of Wellington wealth, of my character's long, hard battle to do well with her life and her feeling of inadequacy when facing her fiancé's rich family, and her bumbling, which could jeopardize her relationship. That is setting, characterization, plot. My "reader question" would be, "Do the opinions of the Wellington women matter to Eric?" and "Will Eric and Shannon marry despite the shaky family relationships?"

Checklists for Balance and Pacing

When you've read a novel that you found unputdownable, that caused you to remember the characters long after you've finished the book, you might want to study that novel again with a fist full of markers or highlighters. Go through and single out sentences that characterize or sentences that are meant to propel the plot forward. (And, naturally, paragraphs that do that.) Motivation is linked to either the character, the story facts or the plot. If, in study, you were to highlight all the characterization elements in pink, all the plotting devices in blue, and all the setting contributions in yellow, the best novels would not have too much of one color and there would be little, if any, unhighlighted material. Additionally, there would be some sentences that would do all three things simultaneously and many paragraphs in which there is some setting, some characterizing and some plotting going on.

Obviously every sentence in every novel can't contribute to those three essential story elements at once, but consider some examples of simple sentences that do accomplish all three things:

1. He hefted the heavy ceramic coffee cup in one hand and fired it at her, missing her head by inches.

(The fact that it is a ceramic cup and not a crystal ashtray says something about the setting; that he threw it must be establishing or confirming some character trait about his temperament; throwing it is a plot action — something happened and there must be a response — action/reaction.)

2. He locked his fingers into the sheer fabric of her silk nightgown and with one powerful jerk, tore it from her body.

3. He stood in the still night, on the open plain, listening for the voices of rustlers to get an idea of how many they was up against. [Dialect, vernacular included in narrative intentionally — this is from *Lonesome Dove*, a western.]

4. She grabbed the phone, retreating into the closet to hide, sitting

across a pair of eelskin boots, a Persian lamb coat tickling her cheek, and called her mother for advice.

Something happens to someone (or with someone) someplace, sometime. That's the rhythm and pace and power of the novel. Consider the alternative: if what was written has nothing to do with the setting, the characterization or the plot, why is it there? I defy you to come up with a reason. That is the single best checklist I can provide.

What if we assume that every sentence, paragraph, scene or chapter has relevance to either plot, character or setting. Is this a perfect book? Nope. Not yet. The novel that does not give appropriate attention to each of those facets is unbalanced and leans to one direction or the other. The characters might be memorable, the setting vivid, but the plot so predictable that you hardly need to read to the end to know what happens. (That you read to the end anyway is no argument for quality—you will not love that novel for long. You will not recall it, think of it fondly, or treasure it as the best ever. You will simply have finished it. Not good enough for this chapter!) Or, you might find yourself barely intrigued with the people in the story, but the setting is so fascinating and the submarine is about to blow up so you rush to the end, but long after you've put down the book you can't remember the protagonist's name. Those might be okay books, but not great books. In which case, not your best study books.

This sort of imbalance not only happens frequently, I've actually read articles in which it is argued that some genres require more of one technical aspect than another. I've heard it said that characterization in romance is the backbone of the novel; the couple must be peopled by complex, fascinating, unique lovers with unusual histories and motivations, stimulating private lives and desires . . . (oh, etc. etc.), but the plot is just boy gets girl or girl gets boy.

Alternately, I've heard it said that the adventure novel or techno-thriller is a busy, busy book; the scientific extrapolation is nearly as complex as science fiction, the countdown factor to danger versus resolution is at high pitch, the action must be continual. And the characterization, therefore, is not so important as the protagonist is driven by powers greater than himself (like a need to save the world from destruction), has a great deal to accomplish in the story, and can easily exist on a few slim traits like courage, stamina and ingenuity.

Bunk.

If the techno-thriller plot is that damn great, I will enjoy the novel that much more if the character is memorable. Tom Clancy bothered to characterize in *The Hunt for Red October*; Jack Ryan is mentioned in the chapter on characterization. Critics cut him no slack, but millions enjoyed that novel and there must be a reason—I cite the unique and painstaking characterization as one prime reason. My argument is that if those lovers in the romance are that damn special, complex, fascinating, multidimensional and memorable, I'll enjoy that novel so much more if the plot is also compelling and not the flat, predictable boy gets girl. Oh, boy *gets* girl—you bet. And our techno-hero *is* busy, pressed to the test and all that. It is not a suggestion that one must abandon the plot-type, genre or elements that are known to work to make the novel work, but rather a suggestion that when you integrate the techniques you make it special. The writer must *use* everything that works in characterization, plotting and setting in balance to create the pace that moves the story and makes it memorable.

Try the highlighting test on a novel you love. You won't have to highlight far before you see some sense of order. The author may begin with one thing—setting, characterization or plotting. At the moment your interest begins to pique, however, you will have found that there are strong elements of all three facets of storytelling present. You may begin reading about an interesting person; there is some character quality or complexity right off the bat that piques your concern. That character has now snagged your interest; it's fair to say that you haven't developed a complete relationship with the character in the first couple of pages, but you are becoming involved. The person is in a place and time you begin to assimilate clearly, dressed in fabrics with textures you have felt or imagined, or choking on dust that images a place you can see and feel in your head. How long can the reader go on with these two elements? A few pages. Perhaps, if the writing is exquisite, a hundred pages. The thing that causes the page-turning *compulsion* happens when the third element arrives on the scene; the interesting person in the interesting place does something or something is done to him or something happens to alter the setting or scene. Plot.

That is not the only scenario; I'm not implying that plot is the element that cinches the reader's piqued interest. The plot could come first. The body could be covered with blood, still warm, lying on the floor of a luxurious penthouse. The gun is still smoking and broken glass lies on the floor under a wall mirror. If people who capture your interest do not soon become involved with this body and begin to exist in this space, you'll yawn and wonder when the story is coming. If there is no character in which you invest yourself emotionally but bodies and rich townhouses cover the pages, it would be about as compelling as reading pathologists' reports.

It isn't a law that these three story components be equally present in *amount*. A pound of feathers weighs the same as a pound of lead even though one takes up more space. Balance the *weight* of the story; don't give your reader two pounds of plot, two pounds of setting, and a half-pound of characterization. The novel that neglects any one of these components falls a bit flat. Likewise, good writers can manage big ideas in brief statements. If you were to highlight an entire novel and found that there was very little characterization, it might bring you to a conclusion. Was that character memorable? Did you think about him/her long after the story was read? Would the story have brought more pleasure with a more fascinating character?

There is a warning about setting details the writer should be aware of. There are people who love to read technical stuff about airplane engines, medical reports, computer components. There are people who love to read about fashion, interior decorating, architecture. People love to read history, philosophy and news stories. Remember that our focus is *the novel*. In the novel something happens to someone somewhere. There is no shortage of nonfiction for people who want to mainline their information. If you choose the Civil War as a setting, involve the people in the conflict and resist the urge to fully educate your reader on every historical detail. Stick to details that are pertinent to the characters and plot.

Giving the Setting a Role

I haven't said anything about setting yet because setting functions, by creating the sense in the reader of "being there." Setting creates a sense of place and time for the story and the people in the story. It far exceeds the need for a good description of the country landscape or the city street. It is not only what is seen, but what is felt, heard, smelled, sensed and tasted. It is tactile sensation and burning taste buds. Setting is both furniture and ambience. It is the way the scene comes to life when the characters respond to their environment. The reader should be able to imagine his nose burning from the noxious fumes or his mouth watering from the seductive aromas.

To say the desert is hot and dry evokes a vague picture. To say the desert is 120 degrees and zero percent humidity creates a more specific picture, but only for those readers who can personally relate to it. But, when you consider the effects of this blistering heat on a character, the picture inflates and comes into vivid focus. It comes to life. When you write about dry, cracked lips, blisters from the sand on the soles of feet, damp clothes clinging to the skin, and a rash beginning to chafe around the collar of a shirt, these are the things that people feel when the heat is terrible. Your reader has either been that hot and relates through memory, or has been hot and miserable enough to imagine a situation that is even worse.

This is setting as it functions in the story. Spike heels that click across the ceramic tile, tennis shoes that squeak across linoleum, or boots that thunk along a wooden sidewalk. Even if a room seems static, still, the writer must feel something going on so the reader hears, sees, smells and feels more when the writer puts a character in the room. The Laundromat is filled with the aroma of fabric softener, a fine layer of linty dust covers the washers and countertops, the thumping and clicking of heavy men's blue jeans in the dryers have the rhythm of a percussion section. The scene comes to life when a character picks lint off her favorite sweater, feels the sticky residue of spilled fabric softener catch the sole of her tennis shoe, raises her voice to converse above the drumming appliances, and wipes the countertop before folding her clean, warm, dry clothes. This is setting when it is alive.

When the writer pauses to describe, pauses to characterize, and then pauses again to develop an obstacle for the plot, the story may move, but it doesn't move with rhythm. When the character responds to her environment, when all the senses are used to create that time and place and situation while something compelling happens to someone important, the story ticks and tocks like a finely tuned watch.

Setting is the element most often abused, ignored or mismanaged. Too many writers think of setting as the landscape, the description, and don't use every sense. You are told about dust, but no one chokes on it. You're told about crashing waves, but the water has no temperature; no conversation is obliterated by the noise. You're told about a splintered wooden banister, but if no one snags a sleeve, it drifts through your head as meaningless flab. This is the abuse of setting; it's there but serves little purpose. The splintered banister doesn't *matter* if it has no function in the story.

When the setting is developed with the same loving attention as a character, it comes alive and has great purpose. When the splintered banister cuts a hand and the injury causes a temper to flare and the flared temper unleashes a fight, the setting has been a factor, the setting has had a role.

How about the storm, the beach or the dark night that has no real plotting or characterizing purpose? I read a manuscript that opened with a woman walking along a beach; other than a brief response to the violence of a mutilated Dungeness crab, the writer merely showed us what the character saw and felt without giving any reason for the reader to *care* what she saw or felt. The writer did all the above encouraged things. The sand tickled her toes, the sun made her squint. It rambled for pages. I stopped caring. Even though the novel was to be about environmental destruction, the walk on the beach was too long, too ordinary, too predictable and had little purpose because no aspect of the plot entered. (Had there been some threat, some environmental destruction, something happening on the beach, I might have cared.) She meant to be setting the stage for some action to come. It was way overset. The fact that the character responded to her environment was not enough to move the story—that character needed to respond to her environment while something happened to her. (I once heard an editor say that she refused to read any manuscript that opened with a dark night or a bright dawn!) If the setting doesn't matter to the character and the plot, it's extraneous.

In some cases setting is virtually ignored. Generic terms are applied to description that is intended to just get the job done, to orient the reader to place and time. He poured a Scotch. He jumped in his car. She spilled her wine. This kind of setting description is like a theater backdrop of painted mountains and blue sky—it gives you a sense of what it's supposed to be, but it has an artificial, unreal feel to it. It's unspecific, bland. There are no smells, tastes, textures or sounds. He poured a draught of Chevis, straight up, into a coffee mug. She meant to slowly lift her glass but knocked it over, spilling a vintage 1945 Cabernet that cost more than her dress. The smell of the leather interior of his Mercedes caused his nostrils to flare in appreciation of luxury. Vivid, specific description that involves the senses and characters does the opposite of ignoring setting—it pays attention to the setting with detail and concern. It's specific as opposed to generic. It's precise.

You can mismanage the setting of the story by not incorporating it with the other story elements, like that long walk on the beach. It's like family videos or home movies—not important to the random viewer. It's usually a matter of not knowing how to blend and organize excellent descriptive material. I heard a good example of this when a friend who happens to be a wonderful writer told me she didn't do setting descriptions as well as another writer. "She writes long pages of description of landscapes and the prose is almost poetic." My friend may be right about the writing and the beauty; I haven't read this description and can't judge. One thing I know is that when a novel contains long pages of description, then cuts to the action, then indulges some characterization points, the story lacks flow. I can't mentally put the character in the place because the character doesn't *respond* to the place. The plot moves, but it doesn't move *with* the environment or the character. I've seen this problem many times and beginning writers seem to get stuck there, and I have a theory about that, too. (In a minute, in a minute.)

Mismanaged setting description stands apart from the story, separate although complete, and therefore doesn't even function as background music. It's like the theater backdrop on the wrong stage. It's like describing the injured and casualties of the Civil War and then creating a scene in which Scarlett washes her hands. This leads the reader to an assumption rather than a conclusion. Showing Scarlett walking through the rows of hundreds of screaming, bleeding men and then crying that she can't take it anymore blends setting, character and plot. Even a mountain view should create a feeling in a character and the mountain had better be pertinent to the plot.

Now . . . my theory about why beginning writers do one thing at a time. First, obviously, because they know it is required to establish space and time for the story and attempt to do so. The intentions are golden, the results brass. Second, because it is damn hard to keep all these balls in the air at the same time. And, you're thinking, she's talking about only three things here when it seems like fifty, including dialogue, motivation, subplot, etc.

So, let's clear that one up right now. Everything winds back to plot, characterization and setting in one way or another. Dialogue either characterizes and individualizes or it moves plot. Motivation is either born of character or plot or is a reason why a character acts or an event occurs. A setting can motivate; a plane can crash on account of a storm. Dialogue can motivate. Subplots are linked to the central characters and/or the central conflict; subplots can show characterization of major characters, can motivate people or events. Obstacles, rising tension, action/reaction are linked to plotting and characterization depending entirely on what happens, who it happens to, who is involved, and what the consequences are.

Back to square one:

1. If it doesn't have to do with the setting in a vivid and involving way, *why is it there?*
2. If it doesn't give the plot forward thrust, *why is it there?*
3. If it doesn't characterize in some way, *why is it there?*

Study this. If it is called motivation, it must be linked inextricably to a character or plot event. If it is called "building tension," it must be linked to the plot or the person. Character histories, value systems, private lives, personal hopes and dreams are meant to build character — if they don't, they're out. Sometimes character traits — histories, values, etc. — cause some plot obstacle. Facts, data, goals, needs, obstacles must propel the plot. If they don't, they're out.

These are the three steps to an unputdownable novel. Balance:

1. A vivid setting that involves all the senses and to which characters may respond with
2. In-depth characterization to which the reader will relate, believe and develop a relationship with those characters so
3. The reader can assume the dilemma of the characters' plot and feel a personal and compulsive urgency to see the story conclusion.

Your Distinctive Voice

Style. This can be discussed in three minutes or three years. The style is the voice of the writer. That's the shortened version everyone understands. It's original because it's yours. When you've read a novel and you admire the style and attempt to emulate it to some degree, the result will still be a unique voice because a little of your own preferred method of delivering a story will be *flavored* by the style you admired.

Some writers like long, delicious, flourishing sentences. Some like crisp, short, clean sentences. Some can blend the long with the short, the elaborate with the crisp. There are descriptive sentences that take a while to say an important thing:

> The sun was still high, sulled in the sky like a mule, but Augustus had a keen eye for sun, and to his eye the long light from the west had taken on an encouraging slant.

There are descriptive sentences that can do a big job in short order:

> The sky didn't move for days.

Both sentences come from McMurtry's *Lonesome Dove*. When an author has a consistent style and distinctive voice, you begin to hear him/her in your head. Most readers, in fact, *hear* the words mentally. (Speed readers and sight readers are in the minority.) Because of this, the most helpful thing you can do for yourself is to read your manuscript into a tape recorder and listen to it. There you will sense the flow, the cadence, the rhythm of your own chosen voice. (Or, on bad days, the lack thereof.) That will be your style.

Of course writers can vary their own style at will, depending on the needs of the current project. The historical novel will be filled with vernacular of the period, frequently with more elaborate language. The contemporary romance could be written with a more conversational style. The techno-thriller makes good use of short, snappy sentences because that tends to imply action and sets a fast pace. Some authors are more fond of metaphor and simile than others.

Style includes the author's ability to break certain rules and be understood. Or, understood even better because of a broken rule. Incomplete sentences. One-word sentences. Pizzazz. This sort of thing has one determining factor and one only. Do it if it works.

One word of advice—leave the stylistic gymnastics to the pros. Sure, an experiment here and there, something a little new and different now and then is no big deal and might even make your story special. There are certain things I've seen done that I never would have believed *could* be done—a four-page paragraph, a one-sentence chapter, a novel written from end to beginning, begun with a twenty-eight-year-old man who is followed backward to his birth. When things like this work, they generally work to profound purpose. These risks were not taken simply to set the novel apart from others but because the specialness of the particular story called for such ingenuity. And incredible skill is required.

Just learn to accomplish a simple suture before doing open-heart surgery.

Practice

What can the writer do to practice writing living, breathing settings, balancing the three basic story elements and developing a unique style? Plenty.

- Sharpen your powers of observation. Sit in a Laundromat and take notes. Include all the senses—what you heard, smelled, saw, felt, sensed and tasted. Do the same in the autobody shop, the hospital, the supermarket, the bus depot.
- Write descriptions for practice. Look at pictures of busy scenes and describe them. Then, put a character in that scene and give him a job—looking for a friend, running from a foe or seducing a woman. Keep the character, setting and plot in balance.
- Make long lists of sentences that accomplish all three story elements, like the man throwing the ceramic cup or the woman hiding in the closet to call her mother for advice.
- When watching movies or television programs, practice isolating scenes in which there is great balance, for example, a fight between adversaries on the narrow ledge of a sixty-story building. Then write it. Catch the feel of the wind, the dizziness, the rage, the gripping fear, the distance of the street below and the little dots that are people.
- Read lengthy descriptions of settings and rewrite them to accommodate the presence of characters and plot devices.

While you're doing these technical things, you are always developing the voice with which you'll tell the story. The more you write, the more your own special voice crystallizes.

Let's say you've done everything asked of you and your novel is at least well underway. You've characterized, plotted, motivated, balanced the story components for the purpose of pacing and rhythm. Let's say the writing is downright lyrical. And let's say something seems to be wrong with the pace, the forward movement of the story.

This has happened to me and to many writers. It even happened to me recently, after I had learned this lesson once. There is a condition that, for lack of a better definition, I call passive storytelling. It can infect the plotting and characterization; in fact, once the writer has begun a series of passive events and characters, the whole thing tends to get worse and worse.

I first noticed this in a novel I loved writing. I loved it so much and wrote it so ferociously, I was rather blinded by the light. I had never created such fancy word combinations. The writing (several people said) was lovely. But there was something wrong; there was no real urgency, no compulsion to turn pages. I had balanced the story components quite well. My agent remarked that the story seemed gossipy. I finally put the manuscript away, giving myself distance from it, and when I reread it months later I saw what was wrong. A sentence on page 157 stopped me: "She was uncomfortable lying to her mother."

There's one of those words I warned you about. Not only that, the sentence did not describe the character. She might have indeed been "uncomfortable," (which doesn't define whether she had a rash or feared the consequences of the lie) but she was determined to lie to her mother.

I saw this again in another place. "Mrs. Ward was not unfriendly, merely cautious." In fact, though Mrs. Ward may have been cautious, she was terribly unfriendly. Cold. Snooty. That sentence came from a character who made an assumption about Mrs. Ward before she knew her. That sentence was written by a writer who was "uncomfortable" with Mrs. Ward's cold, snooty unfriendliness.

These are statements, sentences, that are partly if not entirely untrue, completely unconvicted, and lacking risk. It is an effort to be kind and appropriate and not say (or write) anything too shocking or too revealing. It is missed opportunity and indecisiveness. It is uncertain, unclear, tentative. The cure for this involves more deletions than additions to the story and some major plot and character adjustments. Decisiveness is in order.

The process you've studied about characterization, plotting, motivation and pacing should help you to avoid this pitfall but it is still important enough to elaborate on here. It must be; I've read too many manuscripts in which nothing much happens to vague and confused people. Following are some of the symptoms of this insidious disease. The remedies, I think you'll find, wind back to following the rules about characterization and plotting.

1. Characters with violent mood swings. Just as a character can't be both strong and weak, a character cannot be plagued by temper tantrums and childish behavior one minute, mature and sensible the next. This bounces the character back and forth between extremes and it's like following a moving target. We use the technique of contrast to show that deeper, more subtle side and make sure that characters act mostly on their primary traits. Jack Ryan's brave acts were never born of a core of courage — he was always acting out of desperation, ingenuity or dealing with the consequence of unfortunate circumstances. He got sick or nervous *every* time he was off the ground. James Bond is a different type of techno-thriller hero; he acted on a recklessness and courage that was part of his basic makeup.

When the writer is sure of the primary and secondary traits, characters will not suffer mood swings.

2. Characters who overreact with displays of emotion over relatively benign events. Melodrama. This is linked to the author not being precise about emotions and not knowing what his own emotional response might be. This can also be linked to not getting the facts right. Try this example: The hero has seduced and made love to the heroine; it's a very provocative sex scene. In the afterglow he says, "I didn't realize you were a virgin." She flies into a screaming rage, insulted. What did he say? What he didn't know. Her rage does not directly respond to his statement. He didn't say, "Gee, I didn't know you were such a whore." If the rage is fitting, the hero's words should be patently insulting. Induce the rage with a significant event. Don't put the burden of misunderstanding and overreaction on characters . . . especially if you'd like them to appear to be relatively intelligent adults.

Getting the facts wrong? There is no better example than our chief financial officer from the chapter on motivation. He frets over things that don't exist. It is the wrong emotional response under the circumstances. Change is needed in either the circumstances or the response — they don't match.

3. Conflicting emotions. This is not the same as mood swings. This is a character who can feel two opposite emotions at the same time. Novice writers try this one so consistently that I've begun to think it's

built into the first months of writing as a test. This is the woman who feels weak yet feels up to the task of doing something that requires strength. This is a character who is terrified, but performs a courageous act (not to be confused with Jack Ryan who never planned his brave acts but rather threw up or passed out when he found himself "reacting" in desperation with something he would never otherwise do). This is a character who is solitary by nature, yet very popular and sought after by the ladies. I've read that description dozens of times and I've not yet figured out how solitary men get such a flaming reputation with the women. It is a shy, withdrawn character who's dying to get onstage. It is, really, the subtle difference between contrast and contradiction.

4. Untrue statements or partially true statements. This is the girl who was uncomfortable lying to her mother and Mrs. Ward, who was not unfriendly, merely cautious. In my case the problem stems from childhood when my mother instructed me not to comment on Mrs. Wesley's horrendous shape. We didn't need to *say* she was fat or, God forbid, ask if Omar the Tentmaker was her tailor. Be *nice*. Pulllleeeese. Well, chuck it—as writers we not only have to say she's fat, but also unfriendly and untidy. We have to say she weighs around 340 pounds, hasn't spoken to anyone but her preacher in fifteen years, and smells like the bluish stuff at the back of the refrigerator. Our readers have a right to expect us to be vivid, honest and daring. They can depend on their ministers to be nice.

5. Withholding vital information. The most honest, well-intentioned mistake writers make. They keep telling us to build tension. Don't we have to create questions to cause readers to want answers? Not always. A student recently wrote a cover letter to her manuscript and asked, "Can you see that I have alluded that Blaise is hiding something?" I could indeed. It was so vague and confusing that I became bored with being expected to work so hard to figure out what was going on. I wrote back, "Give me one good reason not to either say, straight-out, he's hiding something or better still, tell me what he's hiding." *That* would build my tension—wondering if he could keep it hidden, wondering if it will come back and bite him, wondering if he'll be damaged.

That writer wrote back to me, a long letter, trying to explain why it was so important that the information be subtle, careful. But the sentence that took my breath away, that made me want to read the novel, that would have driven me forward, was, "He is a vampire." Unfortunately, that telling sentence that fills me with a desire to know more came in her letter, not her book.

The best example of withholding I've ever run across came from John Gardner's book, *On Becoming a Novelist*. He was talking more about developing objectivity than deliberate withholding, but they come from the same place. Sometimes the writer's picture in his head is so clear he doesn't get it all to the page. He mentally fills in the blanks with his research, knowledge, vision, intention, etc. Gardner tells of the short-story writer who believes his description of a bulge under his character's coat is a clear indication she is concealing a gun. But the reader thinks she's pregnant.

6. The sudden appearance of convenient characters or events. This is motivating or proving after the fact. This is weak, circumstantial evidence. This is the woman (from the motivation chapter) who made a phone call to a man she'd never met to tell him that she knew his dead wife and *coincidentally* give the information that his dead wife, who he believed to be terrified of the water, had become an expert swimmer behind his back.

7. Coincidences that are impossible to believe. There is an old saying in fiction — the only coincidence they're likely to believe is an unfortunate one. This is the police detective who *finally* figures out the case at the *exact moment* the protagonist is about to get knifed and just *happens* to get to her apartment seconds before she's a goner. Motivation, again. Planning, again. Things like this can be tidied up in the rewrite.

8. Overuse of clichés and canned, overused statements and responses. You wouldn't succumb to using, "Love means never having to say you're sorry." The cardinal rule here is "Thou shalt think up thy own stuff." The serious novelist must come up with a better line than "His eyes smiled up at her." Grit your teeth and think. Then think harder. Come up with a *better* sentence or a *stronger* piece of evidence. Finding the typewriter with the faulty *e* that actually typed the threatening note has been done a thousand times; one bad twin and one good twin has been on the movie of the week over and over again for years.

My editor, one of the most gifted in the business, Tom McCormack, sent me this quote from my manuscript and this instruction in a recent letter:

" 'You!' he growled. 'You did this to me! You'll pay for this, you bitch!'

"This is, Robyn, a bit 'penny-dreadful,' something hand-lettered in a balloon above a character's head. Since it is a climactic line, it would be pleasant if you could make it a bit better."

When zooming through a manuscript with a killer on the loose and a plot slamming along, one writes what is needed. Then, when one's editor points out that it is rather canned, one looks at that piece of dialogue and remembers hearing it in every single murder mystery movie since one could sit in a theater. Ah, well. Think harder! Come up with something new! Or at least newer!

I didn't come up with anything brilliant, but perhaps a bit better. "He gave up the fight and straightened slowly. He looked at me. 'You,' he said, his voice soft and raspy. 'You wanted to make me suffer. All along.' The voice was calm enough to make me tremble."

9. And also credit to Mr. McCormack for pointing this one out: the hyperactive adverb gland. In my case it was specifically addicted to *degree*: completely, extremely, totally, thoroughly, absolutely, basically, virtually, barely, somewhat, very, rather. And a related cluster of adverbial qualifiers: real, really, a little, almost, not all that much, not too much, not so much. I shouldn't have to give many examples for the student to see how much this can drain a story of its power. "She was pretty likely to use force," is a lot less powerful than, "She intended to use force." Or, "She was thoroughly disgusted," is not as sharp and focused as, "His sexual advances disgusted her." And, of course, "She was a little upset," is like being a "little pregnant." "She was almost angry," is not as good as "Her irritation was cresting into rage."

10. Finally, though we've all done it and it sometimes even slips past good editors, never resort to "There was no way to describe," "No better way to say it," "She didn't know how she felt," "She was momentarily numb," etc. In almost all such cases this merely means that the author hasn't reached for a fresh phrase or a precise description.

To capsulize, to make sure you are telling a crisp, well-paced, convictive story, here are some checkpoints:
- Confirm dominant character traits against character's emotions — be sure the character's emotional reaction *proves* their traits.
- Use true statements with clear meanings and do not avoid risk.
- Do not withhold information.
- Do not rely on convenience, coincidence or overused phrases, ideas or dialogue.
- Reach for fresh, original ideas, descriptions and precise words with precise meanings.
- Watch out for the overuse of adverbs and qualifiers.

If you concentrate on maintaining a clear goal for the characters and closely guard their primary traits against contradiction, your story will have a firm and solid forward movement. Just don't *ever* let the impact of a character trait or a story event frighten you or make you nervous. Readers love impact. They buy it like crazy.

CHAPTER 8

Revision:
After the First Draft

A whole chapter on revision? Oh, yes. Revising the completed manuscript is usually a big job, but not many writers know it. Revising is far more than cleaning up the typos, the punctuation and repetitive adjectives. Not many writers know how serious a prospect revision is because they don't do a lot of it. The new writer tends to become too married to "ideas" they've committed to the story to rip them out and rethink them. And many published writers revise as they go, making a certain significant change in chapter three to accommodate a new twist in chapter seven, but ultimately they finish that draft, tidy it up and pop it in the mail. The revision, the published writer frequently thinks, comes after the editor has gouged his way through the story. I consider that the *final* revision. Cleaning up the manuscript for mailing is like dusting; the revision I'm going to talk about is like spring cleaning.

Maybe not every manuscript needs major surgery, but having a method for checking will at least establish whether yours does. An aside: I frequently think my final draft is as near to perfect as it can be. Also, my second and third final drafts. Funniest thing, I've never had an editor with nothing to change.

First, every novel, without exception, could be made better. I've reread portions of my own stuff published years ago and had that fleeting thought that I wish I could write that story now, knowing what I know. Logically, however, I have no remorse. We do the best we can at the time. Of course there is a point at which you have to put the book to bed, let go of it, let it stand or fall. Most of us let go of it a bit too soon.

Everything that's been mentioned so far in this book is what must be evaluated once again in the rewrite. The story may have felt as though it were going well in the creation, and perhaps it has, but when the manuscript is complete, the writer must begin again and weigh every word. Or, as my editor has said, "Make every word show its papers before it may pass."

There are a few tricks for doing a *good* revision. They are as difficult to do as it is to make a studying writer take notes in Laundromats and practice writing long pages of dialogue recorded from a movie. In other words, these revision tricks work excellently, but few people feel compelled to bother. Everyone wants to sit down, write a book from start to finish and sell it for a million dollars.

Objectivity

Okay, trick number one: Put the novel away for three months. Completely out of sight. Get to work on the next project; throw yourself into something new, something else, keep working, writing, learning and growing, but put the finished novel away. I could say "for a while" but too many writers would consider two weeks long enough and it isn't. Not only must you keep your mitts off it, you must let go of it mentally and emotionally. Get a little distance; stop obsessing the story and the characters.

If it happens that you've asked someone to read the manuscript and give you a critique, don't consider that time period that it's out of your hands as your distance. You will inevitably think about it, worry what your reader will have to say, already start thinking of things you'd change, etc. If that manuscript comes back two or three weeks after you've given it out (and you've been thinking about it all the while) you'll want to dig in and evaluate your evaluation. That isn't the kind of distance I'm talking about. I mean the real thing. Three months of letting it seep out of your head and heart.

What this distance does is give you perspective. When you return to the manuscript you can read it almost as a first-time reader would. Not only will you see the typos and misspellings you slid over when the story was ever-present in your head, you also have the potential to see the larger problems. Next, give yourself a new mental instruction. You're going to attack the revision as though a stranger wrote it. Better still, as though a person you despise wrote it. Pretend it is no longer your baby, your creative genius at work. If you can read the manuscript with the same skepticism as an editor, you'll be able to judge it more for what it's worth than for what you hope it to be. Having read so many manuscripts for friends and students, I now believe the editor *wants* that book to be good. But the editor doesn't know you, doesn't have a clue what your vision of your story is and has no compulsion to make you succeed for personal reasons. Every time I take on the sheaf of papers that I know someone slaved over, made an emotional investment in writing, I say that little editorial prayer: "Please, God, make this manuscript be good." It is so much easier to tell a writer, "I love it," than, "We've got problems." But, my emotional investment, the editor's emotional investment, ends there. It is just a stack of papers waiting to be read. When you are your own editor, as in the revision, you *must* view the manuscript as just a stack of papers waiting to be read.

Organization

As you make your first trip through the manuscript with the purpose of revising, you need a few tools. You'll be looking at a lot of things at once, it's a complicated process, there's always so much to remember, so many details to check, that if you have a pragmatic method to follow it can be a little less intimidating.

As you begin rereading, make three lists. First, *list the characters* as they are introduced, how they are introduced and what you have written regarding their appearance, names, primary traits. This is *not* the character sketch you've been following, but rather the information you read in your novel, as it appears. You can check this information against your character outline, if you have one. One writer I know uses small index cards, one for each character. Such a card might look like this:

Jacqueline (Jackie) Sheppard, b. 1953
    5'4", slight, blue eyes, strawberry-blond hair
    Pale complexion, given to "splotching" or looking anemic when stressed, or when crying. Not robust in appearance.
    Divorced for ten years, attorney specializing in family law, moved to Col. from L.A. in May 1990, two years after the accidental death of her only child.
    Solitary, intelligent, independent, articulate, serious but not somber, well organized, resourceful, worldly and a bit cynical. Strong value is an almost compulsive aversion to dishonesty; hates lies and liars.

This card should contain the information you have written in your manuscript, not the information you have in your head. The above character is one of mine and though I didn't write (in the story) that Jackie was born in 1953, I did fix the year at 1990 and her age at thirty-seven.

The information about her profession, her move, the death of her child and her divorce was given in the first chapter. The traits I listed had been shown in a number of ways: she had lived alone or with only her child almost all her adult life, she worked her way through law school while a single parent, etc.

The purpose of the card or list is that as you see the added traits, tics, contrasts, etc., in your manuscript, you can add them to your notes. Not too in-depth, now. The basic stuff. When you get up to page 340 and Jackie suddenly becomes thirty-five instead of thirty-seven, you don't have to dig back through the manuscript to find the original information. You can make the appropriate correction. Likewise, when you get to page 250 and characterize her as telling a boldfaced lie, you can check that against her trait of almost obsessive honesty and make an adjustment to cure the contradiction. Either motivate the lie so that it's believable or remove the lie and find another device. Or, as I did in my own manuscript, have her leave L.A. to get away from her pitying friends, her sad memories and her feeling of hopelessness after the death of her son, then allow her to make the statement, "I don't run away from things." This earned me an editorial note in the margin that said, "Yes, she does. That's how she got to Colorado." Your character card helps you see most of those flubs before the editor does.

Another purpose of the character lists or cards is to be sure no one is missing. I dropped a wonderful character from a story because in the first draft I didn't have a strong use for him in the end, whereas he was quite necessary to the beginning. I felt compelled to maintain his presence—I had to *find* a job for him. And naturally, you're going to double-check all the traits versus tags versus contrasts and judge them as you read.

The second list is a *time line*. It begins as your story begins.

Chapter One   May 1990; first two weeks in CO.
Chapter Two   June - Sept. 1990; 1st 3 mo. in CO.
Chapter Three September 10, 1990; dinner w/T.
Chapter Four   September 10, 1990, late evening and early morning at T's house.
Chapter Five   September 10, 1990, early morning at Jackie's house, alone, and morning at work, alone.

The time line has so many practical functions that I've used it in self-defense since the beginning of my writing. It isn't very formal looking and frequently is scribbled on envelope backs and scrap paper, but it really comes in handy. The one above is significant—the story is a suspense, revolving around the relationship Jackie has to T., and it's important to the reader that the time frame be clear. She knew him for three months before she had dinner with him, and that "date" was traumatic. There will be many references to his artful manipulations, his method of studied seduction in which he gives her every reason to think he's a perfect gentleman—sensitive, kind, quiet. In fact, he is dangerous. It's important that the manuscript establishes the time involved.

A second practical consideration is the checking of details against time involved. I was just given a perfect example of this by another writer who said she created a scene in which a man told his sixteen-year-old daughter that someone had committed suicide by jumping off the bridge. The daughter said, "I cross that bridge to go to school every day." Her time line revealed a problem—the month was August and the girl was new in town; she hadn't attended that school the previous year. She changed the dialogue to, "That's the bridge I will cross to go to school every day, starting next month."

I've had a scene in which the pregnant heroine felt the baby kick and the copy editor wrote in the margin—"near as I can figure, she conceived a month ago—what's missing?" My transition of time was missing. I didn't move my reader from early summer to mid-fall.

Some novel types have more serious time-line needs than others. Romances that happen fast, from love at first sight to deep involvement; adventure novels in which there's a lot of action in a short period of time or a countdown-type story line. Sometimes your time line involves minutes and hours, sometimes years.

Obviously, your time line shows you whether your character wears snow boots or sandals. Readers pick up on those errors and become annoyed.

You may have scribbled a time line while you were writing your first draft, but for the purpose of revision create a new one from what you're reading in the manuscript now. In every passage in which you see a time reference, jot it down. This is the only way your reader knows when your story takes place; your reader can't see the scribbled time line on your desk.

The third list or chart or graph or outline you need is for the purpose of *tracking the plot*. This will include the basic plot line, subplots, motivations, events and devices. My favorite method for plot tracking that I've used is the outline form. Once again, this is the information you're taking down from your own manuscript as you read it—not a preplan that you have. The only thing your reader will be able to access is the story information in the novel. An example of the outline form is:

1. Ch. 1 — First-person account of the past year of danger and intrigue is being recounted, from the beginning, by Jackie, a single woman who lost her only child and moved to Colorado for a change in lifestyle, a new start, but found terror instead.
    a. She's employed by Roberta Musetta, a sixty-year-old female lawyer who has served the small town for thirty years.
    b. Roberta recommends Tom, the local handyman, to help Jackie with redecorating.
        1. Jackie sees possibilities, for the first time in a long time, in this man.

That is what happened in the first pages of the first chapter, which is sixteen pages long. The actual outline is far more abbreviated because I'm able to remember specific items. I would scribble, "Enter Tom, via Roberta." On the very first page Jackie, narrating, explains that lies and liars nearly cost her her life, but she will only tell it as it happened, from the very beginning, because the manipulations and lies built very slowly, sometimes unnoticeably, like a shadow from noon to sunset. This is my plot plan, which I will follow to the end. On my outline I will list all the "promises" made to the reader. When Jackie has a "dark" feeling about Tom the handyman, I will add that to my plot outline as an event — it is the promise made to the reader that I will follow up on her instinct and come to some conclusion about the man from Jackie's perspective. When I plot that Jackie comes home from a short trip to find that someone has been in her house while she was away, I will list that as a plot device — my promise to the reader that we will find out who was in her house, when and why. When Jackie hides her revolver in the linen closet behind the towels so that whoever secretly enters her house cannot easily find it, it is a plot detail. The promise is that when the gun is sought, it is where it was left. And, when a gun is introduced in the story it is either fired, stolen or something else significant happens to it — it has a *purpose* or it wouldn't be there.

Now, with my outline (map) to follow, when I get to page 350 I will recall that I owe it to my reader to allow Jackie to discover (or come to understand) who was in her house and what the reason was. When someone is in her house three times, she begins to carry the gun in her purse for protection. When these promises are kept, when significant details, events or devices are not dropped from the story, the tension increases.

A fourth option, depending on what type of novel you're working on, is a *geographical map*. I have relied on maps for novels that cover a lot of ground so that my characters don't travel west from castle A to castle

B in the beginning and then east from A to B in the middle. Or, allow for the error of having the distance require one day of travel in the fourth chapter, four hours of travel in the tenth.

These charts, lists, maps and note cards will help you immensely if you *concentrate*. Hopefully you're not going to simply read what's there, but question everything you've already written. While you're charting and concentrating, there are some other things to look at. If this seems like you're doing many things at once, you are. The veteran writer can usually concentrate on two or four items at a time, but will still return to the manuscript with pen in hand for a second and a third read. To this end I use colored pens—my first read might be done in red, my second in blue, my third in pencil. Also, I use crates of Post-It notes in various colors; I loop them over page edges and write on them. Blue might be a character tag—"Show Jackie interact with a client to show her professional side." Yellow might be a plot tag—"Tell what happened to the boxes of her son's memorabilia mentioned in ch. 1." These colored strips stand out better than marginal notes.

Judging the Storytelling

Going through the manuscript again, after you've made your lists and charts and given yourself some instructions for change or made obvious changes (or, if need be, done some rewriting), it's time to judge it for its clarity, consistency, pacing and style. Make a deal with yourself. No mental filling in blanks. It is essential that you read only the black print on the white page. Remember the story from the John Gardner book—the writer thought his description of the bulge under the character's coat clearly indicated she was concealing a gun; the reader thought she was pregnant.

The most important job of the genre novel is to make that all-important emotional connection. If you've written a romance, look at all the romantic elements, make sure you still feel these are romantic events and that your reader will. A slow caress, a kiss on the back of the neck, a provocative piece of dialogue like, "I think you're fooling yourself when you say you'd like me to leave . . . I believe your eyes are begging me to stay."

To have gotten this far you must think you know what works for *you* and what has consistently worked for the readers. So, if *you* think hanging upside down out of an airplane is exciting, risky and thrilling, and if you've written it well, it probably is. Judge each story element for its ability to touch the emotions required for its genre.

Likewise, now is the time to *remove* those story elements that don't contribute or cause the novel to wander from its goal. The checklist for pacing works well here—does that sentence contribute to character, plot or setting? (When your answer is "Well, it's going to in the next sentence," that's not quick enough.) Is there too much time spent developing a mystery in that romance? Is there too much romance in that adventure? Is your techno-hero spending too much time talking to politicians and undercover cops and not enough time hanging upside down out of airplanes? Look for the emotional connection you intended to dominate—desire, vicarious thrill, fear, curiosity—and be sure it dominates and is not diluted by too many other emotions.

Now, clarity. This is more about the words you've chosen to plot, characterize, etc. If you concentrate, if you don't try to "allude" to the reader, if you don't try to implicate, indicate or imply, when you read only the black of the type, all the words necessary to convey the idea will be there. It is important that you say *exactly* what you mean; that you are specific. In any place where you could insert the word "furthermore" to further explain, chances are you haven't taken the opportunity to explain well enough in the first place. Wherever you can make use of "in other words" to explain the same thing another way, you've already missed your best opportunity. All the pretty word combinations in the world will not substitute for a convicted, concise, clear story with clear meanings.

If *you* know Gary is hiding something, if *you* know what Gary is hiding and what impact it will have later, and if *you* know when it will come to light, then you might stand in the way of your own story by knowing too much more than your reader. A sentence like, "You have already trusted me more than you should; I could be your enemy and you not know it," could be a sentence that *you* think says a lot. In fact, a sentence like that without the facts, the information required to make it a very telling piece of dialogue, might mean way more to the writer than to the reader. Give yourself this quiz—have you asked your reader to guess that something is going on, being hidden, predicting danger? In every place that you think to yourself, "Well, the reader should be able to tell from this sentence that such and such is happening," rewrite that sentence! No "shoulds" allowed. You simply can't count on your reader to guess right. Remember, leading a reader to the correct conclusion is paramount—leading the reader to the right assumption is the kiss of death. So, you rewrite the sentence or piece of dialogue to say, point blank, "Now that you've trusted me with so many of your secrets you should know something. I am the woman who had an affair with your husband." Bang.

Is your manuscript doing half the job? Do you read one of your own sentences, knowing all you know, and think what you've read says more than it says? If you have doubts, read the sentence or paragraph to a friend, ask for an impression. Another good test is this — do you feel you should accompany your manuscript with a letter of explanation? Many of my students wrote long letters to me explaining what they had written. If the manuscript, the story, the writing is not wholly clear and explanatory, it isn't done yet.

Next, being certain you're clear and consistent, look for any areas in which you've held back a bit. It is frequently the case, whether in your first novel or twentieth, that you develop stronger and more convictive images of your plot and characters as you work. You begin thinking of characters in terms of their most obvious traits, but then they grow and become more complex as pages accumulate. You begin thinking of your plot as a general idea — man must disarm bomb before it blows — and as characters, subplots, twists and motivations are added, the plot becomes more complex. Now is the time to go back to the beginning and see if certain character traits that became critical to the ending (when your character was more full-bodied and developed) were present in the beginning. This is when you take out sentences like, "She was uncomfortable lying to her mother," and insert, "She was determined to lie to her mother and never considered the consequences." This is when you take out sentences like, "Mrs. Ward was not unfriendly, merely cautious," and replace it with, "Mrs. Ward was unfriendly; she had not spoken to anyone but her priest in thirty years."

The beginning of the novel frequently changes in this regard after you've reached the end at least once. All the time spent setting up the action is usually time spent setting it up in the writer's head. Now that you know everything, how it all comes out and who these characters have become, you can look at that beginning again, trim it to an efficient, informative, engaging opening. Cut to the chase. Only essential information here; save all that stuff about her childhood for later and use it judiciously.

My editor cut my last novel's opening from twelve pages to three! My only regret is I wish I'd seen it first. His sensible remark was, "It will be much easier for the reader to sympathize with her personal feelings and become involved in her introspection when the reader knows her better and begins to care about what happens to her." Well, of course, I thought. I made the mistake of trying to help the reader "get to know her" before she had done anything. Letting her do something through which the reader can get to know her and then reestablishing that action with her thoughts, feelings and history is a more practical order.

Checking Details

Now you must also check your facts. Is everything from the jet's altitude to the type of pistol correct? Is the prison sentence for the convict right? The police procedure accurate? And the motivation facts—would a woman who is afraid go to the attic to check out a noise do so when she has a phone at her disposal? Would a man who knows his lover is pregnant, who wants the baby, decide not to call her for six months? Are all your motivations based on generally accepted human behavior or compared, believably, to the rule to create a credible exception?

Willingness to Change

An essential ingredient in the revising process is the willingness of the writer to cut. Slash. It is not only a process of reappraisal, but a process of action based on that appraisal. It is hard to do; we often become so involved in our stories and characters that every deletion feels like an amputation. Sometimes, though, you can't move forward until you get rid of something—the "problem area" blocks your vision.

This happens to me with crossword puzzles. When I fill the squares with words they tend to become too committed. If I'm struggling for the right crossword and can't figure it out, it usually means I won't get it until I erase and try another possibility to see how it fits. My erasing opens me up to more possibilities than my struggle to see through the existing word. The same thing happens to me with manuscripts. When I'm stuck, when there's a scene or subplot or character that feels not quite right, it's easier to take it out and try another tactic entirely than to struggle to make it fit. The writer who is revising must be willing to make major changes and see how they work. You don't put a bandage on appendicitis. You cut it out.

If you find yourself adding paragraphs and pages to clarify, to make something more obvious, chances are you can go back to the first sentence that appeared cloudy and rewrite it. Or remove it. Anything in your story that appears to require a lengthier explanation probably was poorly explained or poorly organized in the first place. After you realize your foolish and self-indulgent character who "was uncomfortable lying to her mother" was actually better off (from the beginning) as being selfish, cruel and unremorseful, hardly any more explaining will be necessary—now she can *behave* in selfish, cruel and unremorseful ways. And when she behaves, the story moves.

Other Opinions

If you have never sold a novel and have no professional editor to turn to, try having your final draft read by someone. As I've said earlier, revision is not necessarily a onetime thing. You may have already given yourself distance, read with an objective eye, made your lists and graphs and checked the papers of every word before allowing it to pass — and you might do it all again. Depending on the book. I've had novels go so smoothly that twice through the finished draft satisfied me. I had one novel that took three years of my life and was revised so many times that I had five thousand pages of revised and re-revised work stacked up.

About that read. Should you be so fortunate as to have a writer with publishing experience read for you, be sure you can find some connections in their style or subject matter to your own. If you're writing a historical romance novel and your reader is writing fast-paced action-adventure, the suggestions for your work may not be germane. My first romance was given a critique by a woman professor twice my age who eschewed romance and wrote and taught literary fiction. She told me to give it up, it was just terrible. She was frankly more cruel than that. But I am a tenacious devil — I published the novel. I nearly mailed her a copy with a nasty letter, but stopped myself just short.

If you don't have the option of a professional writer who compares in some favorable way to your own subject matter or style, you'll have to look for a regular reader, the kind who buys and reads novels of the type you've tried to write. An acquaintance or neighbor or coworker who reads five romances a month might be a good reader for your romance. Your expectations will have to be geared toward his/her ability. Don't ask for the technical advice that the pros can give; don't expect any solutions or even specific problems. Some of the best questions to ask that type of reader:

Do you like the characters? Which ones?

Did you find yourself bored in any particular place? Where?

Were you clear on time, place, setting, people?

Were there places in which you were confused or unclear?

Those are the types of general questions a reader can answer, but the answers could be as broad as the questions. The thing about readers is that they frequently can't put their fingers on what is wrong, and if it isn't wrong enough to stop them dead, they'll zoom on. It is the difference between implicit and explicit — either the reader couldn't name what was bothering them but didn't much like the novel or they know, for sure, that the repetitiveness of a character's whining drove them crazy. In either case, the answer to the question, "Did you like the characters?" might give you enough of an answer to go to work on. If the answer is "not really," you might probe on. But keep your expectations reasonable. You will ultimately weigh this response for its worth. If your reader is not a professional writer or teacher, you shouldn't look for too much advice.

There are a couple of readers the new novelist might want to be careful of: close friends and relatives and freelance critique services that don't come highly recommended from dependable sources. I have endured both; it cost me valuable learning time.

The first, the close friend or relative, has too much of a personal relationship with you to be objective. They might genuinely love the worst piece of garbage you can type. Or, they might let you know, quite honestly, that it was junk, in which case your relationship could be tinged with hard feelings. One of my *former* friends read an early manuscript of mine. She actually talked me into it because she was such an avid reader, and her critique was that it was almost unbearable, so flimsy and idealistic was the plot, and had I not actually typed it, she would never spend money on such a "Milquetoast" story. She went on to say she thought some readers might, but she was so much more discriminating than the average reader. This critique did not help me, briefly slowed me down, and could have been avoided. Here is a reader who knows how to read, but hasn't a clue how to critique. My reaction to such harsh statements might have been better had I interviewed her, determined her to be of the readership I had aimed for, and had I *asked* her to do me this service. (I say *might*. Learning to accept a critique is tough for the new writer.)

I went in search of a reader for that same manuscript. This was before I knew any professional writers whom I could ask for help. I met a woman who had been widowed for three years, was raising two sons, and my story was about a widow with two little boys. I questioned her about her reading tastes and thought I just might have a shot at getting some real feedback. I gingerly asked her if she was up to reading about a widowed mother; I dearly wished to know if I had captured the emotions of a recent widow in my novel. She was not only up to it, but eager to read. She thought it would be both cathartic and interesting. From her I was given valuable feedback, useful ideas and reinforcement for that which I'd done well in the story.

The other reader to look out for is the one you pay. Sometimes without knowing it. That same manuscript mentioned above went through that process, too. It was my baptism by fire; I learned nearly every lesson on the first few books. A friend had a friend who was an agent, she said. I wrote to her. She asked to see my manuscript. I sent. She scribbled all over it and sent it back saying it needed extensive work before it could be marketed. I thought some of her suggestions were good and didn't realize until much later that all she'd really done was copyediting corrections; there were no plot or characterization comments or suggestions. I wrote her immediately and asked if she'd like to see my other completed novel. She replied that I could send it. I sent. She returned it, scribbled in the same way, with a bill for two hundred dollars. I was twenty-six years old, had two small children, was married to a low-paid military pilot and nearly had a heart attack. I *couldn't* pay the money! I wrote her a pitiful letter explaining I had no idea we were heading toward a service that required payment of any kind. That's when I found out what kind of "agent" she was. She made her living by reading, editing and ghostwriting, there was always a fee, and in special cases when she found manuscripts that were worthy, she represented the author to the publisher with whom she had published two books. (*One* publisher! Two whole books! This is not an agent!) She further explained that she willingly worked on my first manuscript for free because of our mutual friend's recommendation, but that I certainly could not expect her free services indefinitely.

In other words, ladies and gentlemen, I was conned. And, I had conned myself as well, by not getting clear information on who this reader was, what her exact credentials were, and what she could be expected to do. Since the years have ticked by I've found that this particular "agent" has not represented anyone in years, but has earned a few bucks by putting the commas in the right places. *Know* what you're getting; *know* what you're paying for; *know* what that person's experience and reputation is.

Teachers can't always fill the bill either. A friend of mine had a creative writing teacher whom she admired. When it was time to have someone read a portion of her novel, she went to him. Not only did he make her wait six months, not only did he leave town with her manuscript, she learned after the fact that he had never published (although he taught college-level creative writing!), and what he had been writing himself was solar systems apart from her own style and subject matter. He didn't like her novel, couldn't offer much advice, and kept her on the hook for a long time.

There are services with good reputations. Ask for references and recommendations from published authors. Make sure the published author who recommends the reading service has published work similar to yours. Make sure the fee is agreeable beforehand and that there will be no hidden costs. Get a time commitment—will the manuscript be reviewed within six weeks or will there be a three-month wait? Don't mail it to that service if your questions are not satisfactorily answered.

Creative Integrity

One final idea on revision and critique. The writer must be open-minded enough to weigh suggestions against possible improvement and at the same time preserve the integrity of his/her own ideas and intentions. This is a difficult, but important, balance. The less ego involvement you have in the novel, the easier it will be to make hard choices. If the writer's focus is firmly planted on the novel and making it the best ever—regardless of what it takes—that writer will allow himself to *try* suggested changes to see if the story is improved. When the story is indeed improved, the writer's integrity is intact. If the change doesn't appear to work, it doesn't have to stand.

There are two radical fixed points to avoid to have the best mindset to create and revise a novel. Don't think your opinion is the only one; don't think someone else's opinion more valuable than your own. In the middle, between the "I know everything" and "I know nothing" is the ability to give full reign and power to the story, serve it, work for it and allow it to grow into all it can possibly be.

CHAPTER 9

The Study of Fiction:
Learning From the Novelist

D oes it seem a little late in the training to talk about the study of fiction? Let me assure you, this chapter is where it is on purpose. Before you began writing, reading novels was pure entertainment. Oh sure, you might have discussed at great length what you read and perhaps critiqued, dissected and considered the authors' motivations. Now, however, by the action of studying writing technique, each and every mechanical/creative facet in the construction of the novel, you will hopefully study fiction in a new, enlightened way.

As your writing skill level grows, so does your ability to study fiction. How you choose and use fiction will become increasingly more sophisticated. A similar phenomenon was illustrated to me by my son's piano teacher. I love music, but I can't carry a tune in a bucket. Therefore, my music appreciation is limited to whatever happens to please my poor ear. My son purchased a package of classical music on ten compact discs for a bargain. He was proudly playing his "find" for his teacher when I wandered into the room. "Great deal, huh Brett?" I asked. "Well . . . the artists aren't the best, but for the price, I guess it's a good deal," he said. I protested, aghast. Beethoven? Mozart? Chopin? Not the best? "Those are the composers," he corrected me. "Listen to the strings on this one, the oboe on that. And the conducting here is really out of cadence."

Brett, with his experienced musician's ear and his practiced musical ability can not only hear the orchestra at large, he can pick out one bad section, a conducting flaw, a rhythm problem.

This is how the writer studies fiction; we don't just gobble it up anymore, letting it please us where it can. After having studied each technique, understanding its function, and how to replicate it, we can begin to judge not just the whole book, but each individual part.

There's more to the study of fiction than reading it. Let's get that out of the way right now. It was said, early on, that one must read fiction to write it. When the desire to re-create good fiction is born in the would-be writer, the mindless indulgence of enjoying a good book is replaced with the concentrated study of closely examining many books — successful ones, well-crafted ones, mediocre ones, and flops.

I would like to qualify "mindless indulgence" for the Puritans and digress a bit into the difference between pleasure and enjoyment. Reading is never mindless; reading directly involves the reader for the reader must re-create images in his mind, think toward the outcome, make constant judgments, and experience a vicarious emotional connection through characters and events. In viewing a motion picture or television program the viewer's involvement is lessened when the images are shown rather than left to the creative imagination. Also, there are extraneous factors that inhibit or enhance the pleasure of the film — audience reactions, comfort, sensory input such as smells, noise, etc. A truly dumb film could be enjoyed when the mood is right, the audience howls with approval, the popcorn is good, the seats comfortable.

In Mihalyi Csikszentmihalyi's book, *Flow: The Psychology of Optimal Experience*, he discusses the difference between pleasure and enjoyment, enjoyment being that project or pastime that leads to a feeling of having an optimal experience. Pleasure, says the author, is a feeling of contentment when certain conditions are met. One can achieve pleasure from a good meal when one is hungry. It is a pleasure to rest in the evening when tired. Enjoyment, says Csikszentmihalyi, is characterized by forward movement; by sense of novelty and accomplishment. A close game of tennis, closing a contested business deal, having a conversation that leads to the expression of new ideas. After an enjoyable event one has changed, grown and to some extent become more complex.

He lists eight major components to the phenomenon of enjoyment, which is the optimal experience:
- Confronting tasks one has a chance of completing.
- Concentration on the task.
- The task has clear goals.
- The task provides immediate feedback.
- Acting with deep but effortless involvement that removes the concerns of everyday life.
- Exercising a sense of control over actions.
- Concern for the self disappears while paradoxically the sense of self emerges stronger after the experience.
- Sense of time is altered.

Reading can be an enjoyable pursuit, but the committed study of fiction requires more of the student and, likewise, yields more. It's like the difference between observing an event and participating.

What Should You Read/Study?

It is no trick to learn what is popular—there are plenty of lists for that. It can be a mistake to study a novel simply because it has achieved high sales figures. High sales alone will teach a student of novel writing very little. Popular books must certainly be looked at; it would be equally foolish to ignore those high sales figures. Those numbers translate into a novel loved by a lot of people. However, a learning writer needs the best possible instructor, and it is a known phenomenon in the publishing of genre fiction that novels achieve stardom for a variety of reasons. It might be a new trend, it might be the provocative quality of the love scenes, it might be the dynamics of promotion, or it might be timing and luck. Whatever, the study of fiction should not be limited to highly successful novels because there is another publishing phenomenon: the worthy novel written with great skill that didn't reach the heights it deserved. Everyone knows about this bummer—it couldn't be illustrated more clearly than by the number of best-selling authors who have had their earlier, little-known works reprinted after their names have finally been included on a bestseller list.

So, which books are the good ones? They are all good—but they aren't all good for you. We all read and write at varying levels. It is most advantageous to begin with the assumption that every author is doing their best work. (This is not a how-to book for critics, this is for *writers* who want to learn from fiction. It is good to judge, to critique, but the object is not to create a "put-down" attitude toward fellow writers—it is purely a teaching device.) Now you're looking for a book that appeals to you. If you've read a lot about a novel that the critics and other readers consistently agree is well crafted, yet you can't quite get into it, or say you think it stinks, it isn't your book. It isn't your best teacher. Conversely, you may hear a good deal of negative criticism about a type of book or a particular author and you simply don't agree. Perhaps you find much in the novel that works and you're very clear on why and how the techniques work. This book could be one of your teachers.

The best possible scenario, however, is a book that is known to be well crafted, is touted by experts as being superior in its type and you love it. The chances are good, then, that you'll study techniques that are executed with superior skill. The probability is strong that you will be led down the right path; you won't be reading a bad example of workable techniques. Search for those novels that are loved, praised, popular and just your sort of thing.

The selection of a novel is a complicated and personal affair. Begin with the type of story you like best. You like westerns, particularly the frontier story type. Listen to the recommendations of other readers and reviewers. When you've read a few reviews and found that the novel is praised for its depth, its promise of unforgettable characters — heroes and outlaws, whores and ladies, Indians and settlers — if these things appeal to you, you're onto something. Reviewers call it authentic, dramatic and destined to make the reader laugh, weep, dream and remember — and since you understand technique and how it works, you can learn from this. Since it is your favored type, you should feel pretty safe in selecting it.

Reading and studying reviews helps in more than the selection of your fiction. You'll learn a great deal by weighing your opinion of the book against the critics and it's your personal appraisal of the novel that will have everything to do with what you write. Perhaps, for example, you find you love a particular romance that the reviewer seemed to hate. Several possible scenarios come to mind. You might agree with a particular flaw the reviewer noted, like a predictable plot, but you might find the rest of the novel enchanting. In that case you might study aspects of the novel that work well and decide to guard against predictability in your own work. Or, you find you grudgingly agree with the review, the novel *wasn't* that great, but parts of it did prove entertaining. Or, perhaps you come to the conclusion that it was a good novel, well done and the reviewer's tone suggests that the idealism of the romance irked her feminist bent. Whatever the case, weighing your opinion against (or with) the critic will cause you to analyze, consider techniques and develop your own personal likes and dislikes.

You can find extensive collections of reviews at the library. There's the *New York Times Book Review*, *Kirkus*, *Library Journal* and *Publishers Weekly*, to name a few. Additionally, just about every genre has its "fanzine" that contains reviews, ads and author interviews. Booksellers and librarians can help you find them.

Book clubs are a good way to keep abreast of what's being published in addition to being a good place to read descriptions of novels to help you select what you like. I have found book clubs to be one of the cheapest and most efficient concentrations of book news available provided I keep one thing in mind — the book club is trying to sell me that book and therefore will not provide an objective criticism. However, once you've made your commitment to buy a few books (or in some cases no commitment is required) you receive a catalog at least monthly chock-full of book news, all for the price of a stamp. There are book clubs that offer novels in virtually every genre (The Book of the Month Club, Doubleday Book Club, The Literary Guild, The Quality Paperback Book Club) and you'll find these advertised regularly in general interest magazines, membership order forms and all. And, there are book clubs and therefore catalogs for every genre from the Mystery Guild to the History Book Club to the Science Fiction Book Club. These genre clubs frequently advertise in special interest magazines and also (complete with order form) in the material that accompanies the general interest book clubs. Also, once you become a member of one book club, the others all send you opportunities to join theirs— these people are doing nothing to save trees!

To select what you want to read, talk about novels with fellow writers. You will frequently hear recommendations connected with what the novel taught the reader. While readers are sucking the story out of a book, writers are digging for what worked and what didn't.

Finally, now that you've read a lot about a certain novel and feel compelled to read it, here comes the true test. Begin. You will know immediately whether you have any interest in the novel. I remember a bookseller telling a group of writers that readers mainly selected books after reading the first two pages. They gravitate to the section they like best, pick a cover and title that appeals, and then read the opening. I was not at all surprised to hear the readers of entertaining popular fiction did not select their material with the same discerning, pragmatic approach a writer would use. The reader is looking for a good time; the writer is looking for a good resource. (This is not to say you won't have fun anymore, just that you'll be more serious about your fun.) Bear this in mind as you read the opening. Assuming you like it, the study begins.

How to Study What You Read

To start, finish the novel of your choice. Just get the story down. If the writer did his job you have developed a real need to know the outcome. That urgency is no frame of mind for real study so satisfy your curiosity. When the book has been read once, you will have some overall impressions and might wish to jot them down. Perhaps there was a particular scene that you find unforgettable or a character that is so fascinating he will live on in your mind for years. Your first impressions of the novel are extremely important and if you can articulate your own feelings about the story—all or certain parts—you are that much closer to identifying and replicating the techniques in writing.

Now prepare to read the novel again. You won't continue to reread every novel for the rest of your life, believe me. But to really develop a sense for the study of fiction, do this in the beginning with at least your very favorite fiction. In time you will find yourself rereading parts of novels, studying particular techniques, looking for specific things.

Now, your second time through you can pay greater attention to details. Try remembering everything you've learned about each separate component of technical construction: plot, characterization, motivation, setting, dialogue. Additionally, there is action-reaction, rising tension, emotional impact, transitions, the beginnings and endings of chapters, the subplots and the pacing and balance. You will find, early in your study, that some authors are known for tension, some for subtlety, some for plotting, some for dialogue, etc. A few exceptional authors seem to do almost all these things well. Arm yourself with a checklist. The technical steps in this book give you one possible checklist — one that has worked for me and that I have passed on to students. It is by no means the only one. If another how-to book for novelists with a different slant is more to your understanding, by all means, use that checklist. Or develop a combination — perhaps Carr's checklist for character-building is useful but Swain's checklist for plotting is clearer to you than Carr's. You need a checklist that you comprehend for each aspect of the novel.

The object of the study is this: When you understand how a technique works, when you can spot that function in the novel you're reading, you can use the *execution* of that technique in your own novel. For example, one of my friends wrote a romance that I read. The lovers were panting after each other for three hundred pages and I thought I'd faint if they didn't get together. Finally they were united, but there was no sex scene! (I called my friend. I said, "There is no sex in this book!" My gosh!) But the emotion of desire was so overwhelming that I looked closely for how it was done and found lots of ways. The hero was always controlling himself through sheer will; the heroine responded to every little touch with desire and was constantly holding herself back; he couldn't take advantage of her youth, she didn't have the courage to seduce him. On and on. I learned from that romance that one could build enormous desire in the reader by a) contrasting characters like youth and inexperience versus experience and mastery, b) moving slowly through lingering touches and innocent caresses until something as innocent as his kissing her eyes took on positively erotic proportions, and c) letting each subsequent touch or kiss grow more intense than the one before. I took that information to a romance I was writing in which an experienced man "taught" a young woman how to kiss. And it took her *pages* to learn.

As another example, I read a horror novel in which a family had a ghost or other eerie presence moving things around in their home when they were out. It was so disconcerting, they felt so invaded, and they were driven (as was I) to find out what the presence was, what it wanted. I created a killer in a suspense novel that caused his targets to feel frightened and vulnerable by leaving clues that he was smart enough to get into their homes through door locks. The technique was to build tension and fear through the plot actions of the killer.

Study fiction with pen and paper, with highlighters and note tags. Find which areas the author excelled in; *do* write in, dog-ear and highlight books—it's entertainment to everyone else, but it's research to you. When you come across a novel in which characterization is excellent, in which you feel you are becoming intimate with a protagonist and identifying heavily, begin rereading that novel with pen in hand. Note every word or sentence that contributes to character; note in the margins in which way the contribution was made. If you've highlighted a piece of dialogue, note whether that contributed to a basic trait, gave the character depth, complexity, made the character more provocative, motivated the character, defined the character more clearly, etc. Or perhaps that noted piece of dialogue changed the course of the plot or subplot, perhaps it created conflict, heightened uncertainty, or resolved conflict leading to satisfaction.

Read that author's other novels and see if characterizing is his/her strong suit. If so, you lucked out because now you can look at the many creative ways a character can be drawn and the many different situations in which characters can be shown in a deeper, more complex sense. Of course the same is true of plot, of pacing, etc. Once you find an author who seems to achieve a certain technique to a level of excellence, you have something of a map to follow.

Take extensive notes on novels that have taught you a few things. Write yourself a personal book report or review, noting what was special, or what the author was particularly good at. And do, absolutely, keep a list of the novels you've read so that you can refer to it. The best novels you read you remember for a long time; you'll want to go back to them, reread them, notice new things about them that help your own skill development. Keep track of the novels and authors; keep notes on who does what well.

Your discussion of novels with other writers should take on more meaning when you've begun to seriously study fiction as opposed to just reading it. There are big differences in the way readers discuss books and the way writers do. Writers tend to hone in on the skills involved, the development of craft; readers tend to get stuck on scenes or people they liked or didn't like. It is not unusual for a writer with a good eye to find something wrong with a book that is widely loved. A friend of mine who has published over twenty books had this illustrated by her discussion of a novel with a reader. My friend read a novel by a favorite author and was disappointed for many reasons—she found the plot thin and implausible and weakened by a villain who was no match for the protagonist. In other words, the villain could have easily been overcome in the first pages; the obstacle the protagonist faced was too minor. My friend then went to the beauty shop and her hairdresser announced that she loved the novel; she thought it was so romantic, so sensual.

Well, my friend conceded, it had been both romantic and sensual. The reader simply had not heard the engine knocking the way the writer had. The reader, looking for romance and sensuality, found satisfaction. When my friend asked the hairdresser, didn't this bother you, didn't that bother you, the reader admitted there were some things about the novel that were annoying, but not annoying enough to keep her from reading to the end to see if the lovers got together. The reader's involvement in the novel was not nearly as serious and single-minded as the writer's study of it. That the reader willingly overlooked a couple of flaws means that *most* of the novel worked well; it was a romance and the romantic story was solid and well done.

That the above-mentioned novel sold well can be of further help to the discerning student. It is important never to emulate a technique or skill just because it appears in a popular book, and I cannot stress that enough. The student should only emulate techniques and skills that work for a definite reason that the writer fully comprehends. In the above case the writer would not emulate the plot technique in which the obstacle was weak but might closely study the way in which the author achieved the strong romantic flavor. So, ask yourself, if that engine had not knocked at all, how much *more* popular might the novel have been? How much *more* pleasure might that reader have had? The student of fiction can learn plotting from one book, characterization from another and emotional impact from someone else.

This is a form of drop and pick up. You find any weaknesses and vow to avoid them. You find the strengths and vow to do even better with them.

Become suspicious and cynical in your study of fiction. Know your own expectations as you pick up a book. A friend recently told me that she had just read a novel in which the opening was thirty-nine pages of setup without a word of dialogue and a minimum of action. As we discussed it, I learned that those thirty-nine pages had not made her happy or intrigued her. She endured them because it was the fifth novel by a famous writer who had never disappointed her, and once again, despite the thirty-nine pages, he came through with a smashing story.

Swell. He can afford it. When you study fiction, decide for yourself what works because it works and what works because of reader trust, author popularity or just plain differences in personal tastes. Just as I can't tell you what kind of novel to write, I can't tell you what kind is good and I can't tell you what to like. If the story (or style, or characterization, or plot) is not to your personal taste, don't try to write like that! If you're trying to sell your first or second book, you will have to sustain the attention of the editor for a long time; many editors stop reading at ten pages. Any story line that bores you is not worth trying just because it sold *millions*. The story line must first intrigue you; the techniques you employ must be ones you know work and why they work. If you ever get the sense that some writer is "getting away with something," back away from that thing, that technique, that you think slipped by.

Should you find yourself studying a novel in which *many* technical aspects are exceptional, be prepared to go through the novel many times. Not only will you look for specific things, you'll learn how closely those techniques depend on each other in a high-quality novel. Don't be afraid to type up whole chapters of that favored book so you can see how it all lays up on the page. I know of one author who taught herself the technical aspects of craft by copying an entire novel—one that she found to have impact on her, entertained her and seemed to perform almost all of the functions well. *Do* rewrite the ending or write up a summary of that story with a reconstructed plot—this is one of the best exercises in writing.

It's a great exercise to outline a novel you've studied. Book reports for your own use are terrific, but by outline I mean a completely broken down, chapter-by-chapter list of people and events from beginning to end.

1. Chapter One—Lilly and Patricia, teenage sisters and daughters of a widowed boardinghouse owner, are opposite characters and often at odds.
   A. Lilly is the brave and daring one, interested in education and independence.
   B. Patricia is boy crazy, flirtatious, lazy and has an unflinching target toward marriage.
2. A new boarder arrives, a cowboy visiting the Centennial exhibition, and flirts with the girls' mother.
   A. Lilly gets stuck with the extra dinner work because Patricia is once again entertaining young men on the front porch.

1. Lilly doesn't complain because she's already in trouble for skipping school.
3. A fight between Patricia's young men erupts and the new boarder must step in and stop the fight. Patricia's mother is just beginning to see that she hasn't taken a firm hand with her daughter and Patricia is surely headed for big trouble with men.

A summary of the people and action from beginning to end, surrounding the basic premise at the center of the story and marking the introduction of new characters will show clearly how the story expands and the characters come into focus. It also helps to show the rhythm of the book, how an obstacle is introduced, built up, intensified and eventually resolved. In the above example, a novel of mine titled *Woman's Own*, Lilly's daring and independence dominate the story, but it is Patricia's lazy selfishness and classic manipulation of men that provides a major subplot.

You'll have to eventually learn how to capsulize a story, so write a synopsis that highlights the central points and major characters, the story's main goal, the theme or enduring message, and importantly, the feelings it evokes in you. Write it in the most entertaining way you can; *write it to sell it*.

You should be able to write a complete and entertaining character sketch of a prominent character; his/her basic traits, history, motivation, value system, secondary traits and tags, idiosyncrasies, contrasts and what drives him/her. If you believe the author did it well, if you feel you know this character very deeply, and if you consider yourself a writer (even a beginner), you should be able to write that character description yourself. And write in a way that would cause another person to want to read about that character and his/her exploits.

The hardest (and most beneficial) novels to study are those in which it appears almost everything is done well. But there are other novels to study closely as well — the novels that don't do everything for you. Take a closer look at that book that was established as popular, sounded (from the ads, reviews, book jacket) like something that would appeal to you, yet fell short. First, you'll see the flaws. That's the easy part; once you've seen them, you know enough not to repeat them in your own work. Perhaps there was a lack of motivation or a weak plot line; perhaps the characters didn't evoke any sympathy in you.

You're not done with that book yet. The flaws may be glaring, which is fine if you've learned something. Can you now find those elements that *did* work? This can be critically important to your own novel writing. There is always a reason why a novel is popular! Always, I insist!

I've been talking to other writers for years and years about bestsellers and what makes them. I've talked to editors and agents and booksellers. The conclusion that I've come to is that it is far easier to determine why a book did well, than to figure out why a wonderful book did nothing. There is always *something* in that popular novel that blew somebody's skirt up. It may be a quality not to your standards, perhaps a totally idealized love affair that you found contrived and dopey. Would a close look show that a lot of people like dopey, contrived romances? No! A close look might reveal what emotional connections readers make.

I've read whole novels that, in the end, I found little to recommend them, yet millions of readers loved them. Sometimes the features that drew readers seemed thin to me, but useful just the same. In one such novel I found two features that I believed caused popularity. The first feature was a highly energetic and admirable heroine; she seemed never to sleep, she conquered every problem, she was driven by ideal values that she refused to compromise no matter what the consequence. I remembered that readers identify closely with personal conviction, with unshakable moral standards. She was highly admirable. The other feature was the author's ability to brush up against a social issue without getting in too deep—issues that, when handled singularly, require a very deep understanding and knowledge to be convincingly approached, like racism. But I was reminded that not everyone wants an intense look. Many readers understand that life in general is affected by such issues, but at different degrees. A young black college student in Mississippi in the fifties is affected in a very different way than a thirty-five-year-old white businessman in St. Paul. This particular author had developed an ability to use controversial issues as subplots, giving her admirable characters a chance to behave admirably while the main plot trooped onward. Main plot would be romance, getting a man and woman together. Subplot would be something like a black coworker of the heroine is discriminated against on the job. Heroine takes a stand, quits job, and is broke, making her even more vulnerable than before, making her likelihood of getting the guy more at risk.

The important thing about the above example is not what I found— this isn't a lesson in what specific plot ideas or character types work. Lots of plot types and many different character types are popular. The important thing is that I managed to find a couple of "working techniques" in a novel I wouldn't recommend. I take a lesson here that admirable characters draw readers, and controversial issues give novels substance, and using issues to build a character's value system connects with the reader. When I use those lessons I hope to use them with more skill. If those two lessons are pertinent to my work, I will do my best to pull them off more expertly than that author did.

You can learn from a variety of different types of books, and it's essential that you're honest with yourself. Don't hide in the closet — don't read hundreds of romances and pretend you only read nonfiction. Discover, honestly, what you like, what works for you and what works on you. And let me tell you about *Lady Chatterley's Lover*.

A woman at a writers' conference was making something of a loud spectacle of herself in criticizing what she called pornography. She referenced *Lady Chatterley's Lover*, which I had read some years ago. She thought the novel pointless, disgusting and a good argument for censorship. At one point she referred to a particularly "dirty" scene that had something to do with wildflowers. I actually remembered that scene. I went home and dug around for the book and paged through it, looking for the wildflower scene, one of many that had set the woman off on her adamant criticism. I found it. After two hundred pages. She had read the entire book; every blasted word. Why? So she could be disgusted? Of course not! It's like the panel of judges who has to see the porn movie for the ninth time to be sure it should be censored! There was *something* in that novel she loved — it could have been the erotica, it could have been embarrassment. The woman is certainly not obligated to write erotica just because she has read it — nor is she obligated if she's enjoyed it. But the very idea that she can say one thing and do another will not build a good writer. *Be honest with yourself*. If, perchance, you have read some provocative erotica and enjoyed it, use that skill in your love story in a fashion that does you credit. When you find something that works for you, don't eschew it. Notice it!

One more thing. It's great to find a point or two that work in a novel you don't particularly like; it is prudent to find the pluses in what you study. It is more expedient and logical, however, to study fiction you don't have to put through a sieve to get a chunk or two of good stuff from. When I study, I have to look for novels that have a great deal to recommend them.

The student of novel writing learns to read novels that aren't favorite types, too. I frequently read novels I *must* read — a bestseller that is being talked about, a novel with a unique style, plot or something important to know even though it isn't really my type — a novel of a genre I generally avoid but is touted for its praiseworthy characterization or something. I read to know what's being published, to learn about technique, and in search of new ideas. I run out of time to read my friends' novels, which would be fun for me. Study is not always pure fun. I have read horror novels just to judge the pacing and tension — the fear factor.

Understanding how it works and seeing it done well can help me to produce some similar emotions in a dissimilar story. Throughout the years, and with my list of novels I've read handy, I find which authors handle transitions beautifully, which are known for dialogue, for cliffhanger chapter endings, for characterization. When I can't find that book that "does it all" I might read a techno-thriller to judge the action, a good romance to study characterization, a multigenerational family saga that covers fifty years to study transitions, a horror novel to look closely at heart-pounding terror, and a fantasy to see how a writer convinces a reader to suspend their disbelief. Then I might get back to work on a mystery, armed with some of the best examples of the best techniques.

Emotional Impact

It's my personal opinion that most successful genre novels can trace the bulk of their popularity to the emotional impact the novel delivers. The impact of its type. Delivering emotional impact is a technical writing device that can be spotted, tracked and outlined as much as characterization as a technique can be. You judge the success of the writer's skill against the emotional response you experience while reading, then track the specific words, sentences and scenes that create that response in you. It's very important that the studying novelist *see* this technique as well as *feel* the emotional response. The successful horror novel is really scary, the successful techno-thriller is filled with heart-stopping narrow escapes, the best-selling romance builds the tension of desire to a fevered pitch. I personally believe that's one reason a techno-thriller can be successful even when the characterization is flat or a romance can earn a fortune even when the plot is predictable and typical. I also feel, strongly, that when the writer pays attention to all the techniques and fine-tunes all the details, those novels would be twice as successful.

Studying Details

There are a few other things you can get out of your study of fiction. One is listing word combinations, descriptions and words you haven't seen before. Don't count on simply remembering those drop-dead lines or piercing descriptions. In some cases you can use them in your own work, but in most cases you can take a lesson, do a little adjusting with your thesaurus, and come up with your own drop-dead lines. It is from these notes that you come up with the way to say that the businessman had an office with a big desk—"The dark mahogany desk dominated the room." Pat Conroy's whale with a "tooth the size of a table lamp" might be just the inspiration you need to describe a pregnant woman's swollen foot that looks like five Vienna sausages sticking out of a cantaloupe.

I have begun to use large index cards — they fit inside hardcover books just right, are about the size of a full page, and I can get lots of memorable descriptions, word combinations, insights, etc., on one if I write small. I have piles of them, covered. The first time I come across something I'd like to remember, I get out a card, put title, author, and date on top. Generally, if I find one thing I don't want to forget, I'll come across many. Here's a sample of notes I've jotted:

1. disingenuously
2. the smell of hot linen hangs pleasantly in the air
3. And yet. And yet.
4. Only true love can justify such lack of taste.
5. her hair anyhow
6. preposterously worn out by fear
7. moved with all the speed of bureaucracy

You can see what an odd lot that is. Sometimes it's a word I need to understand and determine whether it's useful in description. Sometimes it's an idea I want to give some thought to — can one be so in love that tremendous lack of taste can be overlooked? Sometimes it's a description like "hair anyhow," sometimes a stylistic technique that worked on me — And yet. And yet. Sometimes it's a memory — I remember loving the smell when my grandmother ironed, which she did constantly. I am caused to remember other things that I can use: cracked linoleum countertops, Ivory soap, Grandpa's shaving cup that he'd let me make the suds in, ketchup sandwiches. Really.

Your lists have so many possible functions. You can get the exact wording you need. You can get close enough to the exact wording you need so that some adjusting and word changes will make it perfect. You can lubricate your own imagination and creativity, deepen and expand your own thinking.

Two points to remember — important ones. First, if you don't write down the precious gems, if you trust your memory, you will lose valuable research information. You may not forget immediately, but you will forget eventually. Even if you never forget the line, you could forget the source. A good writer won't risk it.

Second, do not take another writer's words. They are hard come by; thinking of this stuff is torture. It isn't free and it isn't yours. It is theft, though you won't get in serious trouble for using "Her hair was anyhow." What will happen instead is you will become lazy, you won't get better at finding the perfect, original, creative, drop-dead line. To use the ideas of other writers to seed ideas of your own is clever and creative; to take what another has worked for is lowdown.

CHAPTER 10

Creativity:
Becoming a Writer

I s this the chapter where I tell you to plumb the depths of your inner being for a crucial, creative message? The point at which I tell where to find the inner workings of the writer's muse? The final word on the little secret the published writers are keeping from you? How to grow creative talent where the weeds of errant thought choked all potential ideas?

Nope.

In most how-to-write books this chapter comes first. It's the place in which the teacher revs up the student's desire by inspiring him or her. Once you're inspired, you think you can do anything. Once you *think* you can do anything, you usually do remarkable things. But, this chapter comes last for a reason. If none of the work involved in the first nine chapters of this book appeals to you, if you found several techniques and practical steps you think you might just as easily skip, if there is no powerful urge to study, this chapter will do you no good. If you're not just a little awed by the commitment and work required, you might think it's easier than it is. It is by-God work; work that leaves you brain-sprained, sweaty and feeling like you're just recovering from a serious illness. Writing fiction is hard work. It remains hard long after you've discovered your own creative talent.

So is creativity hard work. It isn't very often just *there*. It is usually *sought*. And it isn't a little spark that surprises you with it's sudden appearance; creative thought must be tied up, pinned down, wrestled around and shaped into its most useful form.

I watched a talk show with four best-selling authors. I had read them all so I was nearly feverish with excitement. I was entertained, but something kept gnawing at me; something was amiss and not satisfying. One question was, "What advice would you give aspiring writers?" to which three of the four answered, "You must have the guts to try it, to pursue it." Yes, I thought, you must have courage. The risk of spending so much time and energy and perhaps failing stops many people before they even buy a ream of paper. But I remained troubled by this advice.

Eventually I figured it out. It was my argumentative self; this takes so much more than guts! It takes enormous talent, incredible commitment, an awesome amount of hard work and concentration. These four best-selling authors had all experienced their first bestsellers with their first published novels! They didn't discuss writing, what it takes and what it's like, the way my friends and I do. One of the authors had worked for twenty years writing for television before he attempted a novel; that's an awful lot of experience. Two of the authors had written a good deal of nonfiction and short fiction and brought incredible talent and experience to their first published novels. The fourth had published scholastic materials prior to her bestseller and her idea set an entirely new trend—a never-done-before type of book that caught on in a major way. Not many writers approach the craft with vast amounts of natural talent and ability and luck.

The rest of us, my friends, are going to start with a lot less than they did, work a lot harder to get not quite as much, and pay our dues. It is an uncommon thing, perhaps an *unknown* thing, to take a notion to write a novel with little or no experience and training, do so, and sell big. For those who think they will, or can, or have, I have nothing more to say.

Writing is, of course, an art form. It is, naturally, born out of imagination, instinctive creativity, visionary fantasy and lots of other hocus-pocus inner talents. There is positively no telling whether or not you have "it" before you have had sweat. Novel writing just will not work the way the "Draw the picture on this matchbook to see if you have natural artistic ability" works. (Not that that actually worked for anything more than getting an enrollment in art classes.) If you've been working seriously for six months and have not had any professional encouragement, have not had any writers, teachers, agents or editors tell you that you're really onto something, it is *not* a foregone conclusion that you're a creative wasteland. Likewise, you may not discover whether you have "it" after six years. "It" depends entirely on "you." We each have our own learning and developmental pace. I discovered that I had some talent for writing after three years and three completed manuscripts.

You make creative choices every day of your life. How you dress, decorate your house, travel to work, raise your children, manage a relationship with a mother-in-law who doesn't like you, cook your meals, and make your investments depends on your creativity. Some people *are* more right brain-oriented than others; to some two plus two must equal four or there is not enough logic to support the choice — but some of us say, "Two *what?*" I happen to have a mixed marriage — my husband, the trained engineer and pilot, relies largely on logical concepts to make decisions — he has the left brain. I have the right; logic doesn't matter to me when the baby won't stop crying after four hours — I begin to think creatively. If my left-brained spouse decided to write a novel, he could probably do it if he loved the idea and were willing to work very hard. And he would undoubtedly write the kind of story that would depend heavily on logic, systems, cause and effect. He happens to like techno-thrillers or futuristic extrapolations. I tend to rely heavily on emotion, on instinct, on what I know of socialized human behavior.

We're not stuck with what we've got. It is not as though you were born with ten ounces of creativity and what you start with is what you'll have in five years. Or ten. You have no way of knowing what you've started with — and however much, you can fertilize it and it will grow. You can develop artistic instincts, creative imagination and visionary thinking. You develop it by *doing it*. And you *do it* by the steps in this and other writing books.

Your personal ability to create is dependent on many techniques and external forces. The first step to making room in your head for the creative experience is to get out of your own head a little. The longer you run around inside your own head, relishing your own experience, the longer you are kept from connecting that experience with the rest of the world. Your divorce is not that interesting! Your father was a lovely man, but he lacks the conflict, tension and provocative thrust of a protagonist. All you went through to build your company from one rental car to a national car rental chain is fascinating to your friends and acquaintances, but is it fodder for a novel? Not without a lover, spy, murder or conspiracy.

A prospective student called me to explain that she wanted to enroll in the course but she had one problem. She didn't have time to do the novel report. She was hard at work on her novel, had been for years, and couldn't take the time to read a novel now; she'd already read enough novels. I am no longer surprised by the number of people who think they will write a novel without reading them, but I patiently suggested she do a report on a novel she'd already read. She said she hadn't read one in nine years. *Her* story was not dependent on anyone else's novel.

She may indeed have many creative ideas, but just any idea doesn't necessarily fill the bill. Ideas that work in fiction have to have two major qualities. The ideas must be connected to issues of universal concern and flush with emotions experienced by all of mankind. Then, the ideas have to be broad enough to contain the elements of fiction — conflict, tension, entertainment, etc. Divorce might be an issue of universal concern, the emotions of grief and longing might be shared by all humans, but for this plot line to work there must be all the elements of the novel within. There must be a goal, a need, a plot line. There must be interesting characters with big obstacles. There must be something new, special, different and provocative about this divorce.

Developing creativity and expanding the imagination requires discipline. The creative mind can be trained. All the tools given in this book so far can be used in the training. Studying fiction to understand precisely how the technique of motivation has worked for other writers is the lubricant to your own ability to dream up the most appropriate motivation for your story. Practice writing scenes that may or may not appear in your novel to get the knack for pacing or characterizing is the grease through which your imagination begins to slide. Mentally revising a published novel's plot line or ending constitutes an idea.

This requires more than sitting around thinking about your divorce, or your father, or your business success. It requires the study of fiction to see which ideas have traditionally worked. Universal themes include sexual love, sibling rivalry, escape from a threat or danger, competition, grief over loss, overcoming obstacles to achieve success. Through the study of novels you've expanded your imagination to include some outside forces; you're no longer just running around inside your own head, alone. Through discipline you use the information you have about issues, themes that work, to reject some ideas and expand others. After reading a hundred novels you see which story components and techniques have made the issue of divorce entertaining.

Through discipline you determine whether the story that's been running around in your head bears any resemblance whatsoever to stories that have been published. Now your father, who was resourceful and imaginative, becomes a detective — the tribute is to the larger issue and emotion. It began as personal, it grew through the creative process into something universal. This is when you throw out the experience of your divorce and focus instead on the pain of loss and the ache of desire — the larger more universal concept — and write instead about a divorced woman who falls in love, this time with the *right* guy. Or, as I read Sue Grafton got her start, your fantasy of killing your ex-husband becomes a murder mystery.

The steps in this book are the process by which you know whether your idea interests anyone besides you. You learn how the techniques work in fiction. You emulate the techniques. You study fiction and force yourself to reconstruct your ideas into concepts that are broad enough to hold the techniques. Since those concepts have worked in fiction they can work as well for you.

And now you add *yourself*. Your personal emotional response to an issue that you know is of universal concern. You take an idea that can support the components of fiction and search your brain for the something special that makes your novel slightly different from the usual thing. Now you insert a character who does not begin as classically handsome and masterful into the romance, giving him much to overcome to win his lady. Now you can take the lawyer who never practiced anything but tax law and put him in a criminal situation that forces him to become a detective to save his own life. Take an idea that is dependable and with a bit of alteration, make this tried-and-true formula different. Special.

Let me tell you about Mary and the issue of being excluded, left out. She was only eleven and the only girl in her sixth-grade class who wasn't invited to the first boy/girl party. It devastated her; she cried her little heart out. She wanted to go so badly that she tried every angle; she even asked the girl giving the party to include her, but the girl coolly replied that her mother had set a limit and the limit had been reached.

Well, Mary thought she'd gotten her big break when Melanie called and said she couldn't attend the party because she had to go to her grandmother's house. Melanie suggested that Mary could attend in her place. Mary called the hostess to suggest this, but the little hostess replied that her mother had firmly insisted, no more!

As if she wasn't hurt enough, one of her friends called her to tell her all about the party. Poor Mary, crushed, sobbed to her mother. "Mom, Mrs. Smith said it was a good thing that extra little girl didn't come to the party because she had just enough chocolate eggs to go around. Oh, Mom, I wouldn't have cared if I didn't get a chocolate egg! I just wanted to go!"

That little girl's name wasn't really Mary. That was my little girl. I still ache when I think about it; even my husband cried real tears for her. I am often reminded of the need to belong, of the cruelty of children, of the hopelessness one feels when excluded. This is how the novelist adds herself to the story. After examining the many ways in which this issue and these emotions have been used to make fiction, I will bring my own personal feelings into the story in my own unique way. I probably won't write about an eleven-year-old girl who doesn't get invited to the party, but I did write a novel about a young woman who, though pretty, smart and capable, had no young men pursue her because she was too different, too independent. When all the other young ladies had dance partners, she stood alone. When all the other young women were planning marriage, she had no one. And because she wanted a family, she felt a deep sense of loss.

Creativity is linked to willingness. Test yourself. Are you willing to see that idea in a larger context? Are you willing to test that emotion against the emotions in successful fiction? Are you willing to risk personal growth or are you fixed in place? Are you willing to learn and take instruction? Are you willing to try a new way, a different approach?

Something inspired you to write a novel. It doesn't really matter what. Some writers are born out of a desire to re-create fiction because reading fiction gave them pleasure. Others thought their personal story so vital it should be shared. Still others wished to honor a beloved person, while their counterparts wished to punish someone who had damaged them. You'll always remember what gave you the bug even if you've traveled far from that place.

Now is when I tell you to plumb your soul, the secrets of the writer's muse, etc. It comes to all working writers at different points in time. I remember when it hit me. Exactly. This was my creative epiphany.

I was standing in the kitchen of an Air Force base housing unit. One kid was playing in the mud outside and one was hanging on my legs whining about something. The phone hung on the wall, the linoleum was stained and cracked, the moving van would arrive in two days to take my personal belongings to perhaps another Air Force base housing unit with perhaps worse linoleum. It was Wichita Falls, Texas, July 1977. The mailman had just delivered a large, brown envelope. Advances from publishers do not take up such space; it was my manuscript returned. Again.

My third completed novel had just returned for the third time. I felt terrible about it; obviously I was kidding myself. By now, after three years of full-time struggle, had I not come up with a publishable novel? After all the study, writer's critique groups, practice, reading? Not yet?

So, what are you going to do, Robyn? By now you've surely gotten the message. You *think* you can do it, but it remains undone. You *desire* to write, but no one desires your writing. You have studied and worked, but something hasn't gotten through. You've asked in so many ways, "Do I have 'it'?" and you just can't get a straight answer. Or, at least not the answer you want. So, what are you going to do?

"I'm just going to write anyway," I told my husband. No matter what they would say, I decided to keep on. I'd try harder, sure. I'd work harder, yes. But it didn't matter whether the publishing world agreed with me this year or in ten years or not at all. I *liked* writing. I couldn't wait to get the kids down for bed so I could return to my novel-in-progress. What a far cry from wanting them in bed so I could watch TV! I couldn't wait to get up in the morning so I could hurry through my chores, get the little ones involved in something I could monitor while typing at the little dining room table. How I hated to be interrupted by the phone. How I resented laundry and cooking when I could be finishing a chapter! How I loved falling asleep to thoughts of tomorrow's plot problem and how I would fix it. I was completely unwilling to give that up—that total obsession that fed me so thoroughly.

That was the most freeing moment of my career. I would write anyway. Of course I wished to be published, but I wished first to be allowed to write. Of course I wanted a bestseller, but I wanted first to have that daily feeling of challenge, struggle and creativity. I would be lost without writing; my mind is too active to be satisfied with all the daily ho-hum nonsense. I can be the kindergarten mom just fine, just not full time. I can make a helluva meatloaf, starch a shirt, wipe a nose and drive a car pool, and I *still* have so much mental energy left over. And making up stories feels so good. When I do that—when I write—I am participating in my own life, in my own creativity, and I feel as though I've grown, made myself better.

Fun.

People search for that thing that is, to each individual, fun. I believe that is the fulcrum on which all the study, creativity, ability and discipline is balanced. For me, writing was so much fun, however difficult, that I meant to pursue it to the end. Unsnagging the snags, getting the point, studying what worked, creating scenes and developing people was hard, and when I thought I'd done it, was so overwhelmingly gratifying I could not give it up.

Did I have fun every hour of every day I wrote? Heck no. Do I now? Come on. What I have is enjoyment that is sometimes joy. I have challenge, concentration, immediate feedback as I read what I've written, a sense that my self is not a part of me though I emerge as a larger self, a sense of time alteration, a distraction from everyday, ordinary concerns. I sometimes don't notice how hard I've worked until I realize I forgot lunch; sometimes I have lunch at 10:00 A.M. because I'm thinking so hard and still can't come up with the right sentence or idea or transition. But always, when I finish something that I've finally mastered to the best of my ability, I am filled with the thrill of accomplishment. I just keep going back for more.

Fun is the writer's muse. Some writers call it need; I've never needed to do anything I didn't think was fun except pay taxes. I might *have* to mop the floor, but I don't feel driven —I feel like the consequences of not mopping it outweigh the tortures of just mopping it fast and getting it over with. No, I am driven by the fun factor. When I stop having a good time, I'll quit. When I struggle and feel I've accomplished nothing on Monday, I figure it'll come on Tuesday. When Tuesday passes without my fun meter blinking, I look to Wednesday. It *always* comes eventually—that feeling. Yes! *That's* it! Why didn't I see it sooner?

I put myself through a lot to get to the fun part, but is this any crazier than running a marathon? Those people think they're having fun. Or weirder than rebuilding car engines?

I'm deadly earnest about my fun. I'm not frivolous. I take it very seriously. I know that when I work hard, when I stretch, when I feel I've done it, I'm going to feel really good. I have nonwriting friends who work out, decorate houses, skydive and play tennis for fun and they're as serious as I am. While I can't imagine jumping out of an airplane for fun, some of my friends can't quite believe I'd get so involved in my writing that I'd miss a meal.

I don't know if all writers have as much fun as I have. Or if they're having the *kind* of fun I'm having—with as much work as it is, it must sound like practicing bleeding. One of my friends who is hard at work on her first novel groaned a lot through the first several months I knew her. She kept saying she didn't know if she was actually doing "it" but she was trying her hardest. Then one day, out of the blue, she said, "I don't care how long it takes, I'm going to get this right." And I asked if she was having fun. She said something like, "Fun? You call this fun? I don't think it's fun, but it's what I want to do."

I can't tell you when or if you'll stumble upon this kind of finality—the assurance from within that you're pursuing something you have chosen and feels right. I'm not always the most encouraging fellow writer. I don't always say, "Come on, you can do it."

Let me tell you what I told Charlie. Charlie, brilliant man, gifted writer, has been my friend for over ten years. I read his first novel and it was good. So were the second and third. But Charlie was easily discouraged; a couple of rejections and he'd store away the manuscript. Five full novels later he called me and asked me to make the final decision for him. "If you think I have 'it' I'll try once more. If not, I'm going to quit." I told him to quit. I told him he was a wimp. This is not only a difficult undertaking, but also a tough, competitive business. If *he* didn't think he had "it" then he probably didn't. Well, Charlie didn't quit. I don't know what kept him writing; somehow he just kept writing. Something about creating a novel had snagged and held him. His sixth finished novel sold . . . and sold bigger than anything I've ever sold. And he was asking me to make a final judgment? What a lovely dope.

I know writers who are frustrated by the plot flaw, worried about the motivation, concerned about the love scene. All the writers I know who are still writing may not admit to having fun, but every last one says he or she is doing what they want to do.

If you are writing and it makes you happy more than it makes you unhappy, I suspect you're on the right track. If, while you are writing, you open yourself to the possibility of new techniques and ideas, have a willingness to study and enlarge your vision, I bet you'll eventually publish a novel. If you feel that you've grown, personally, from this endeavor, then you've received the greatest gift in this study.

By the way, that manuscript that came back? The one that caused me to have my creative epiphany? It never came back again. My next mailing was to an agent who took it on and it then sold to the thirteenth publisher to read it. It collected quite a few rejections, but it did very well in the marketplace. And I've had quite a few rejections since, which is the nature of the beast. I think I made the right decision — to write because it pleased me.

Writing changes people. You'll never wait in an airport the same way again. People have become more interesting, ordinary situations take on extraordinary meaning. Noises in the dark of night tend to take on exaggerated dangers; a half-smile from the man at the next table could inspire days of romantic fantasies.

Even those people who have always had wild fantasies find the act of writing, the effort of thinking out imaginary situations on paper, increases their imagination. Because we writers are constantly in search of the next character or plot idea, every little thing we encounter is just more fodder for the story. Because we're constantly using our imaginations, our imaginations are all the more ready to be used.

This is inspiration. It isn't something you trip over because you're not watching where you're going. It is the one thing that you've been searching for; after you've thrown out five ideas as not good enough, it is the sixth idea. The one that feels right. So many varied things can inspire the novelist's work, the list is positively endless. The next great idea can come from the newspaper, a television program, a favorite novel, a situation you observe while sitting at the bus depot. Your next great character can come from someone you saw at the beauty shop, a story you heard about your neighbor's mother, a television commercial you happened to see.

Inspiration isn't something you wait for. It isn't standing out there, just barely beyond your reach. Inspiration is that thing that you constantly reach for, that wriggles out of your grip most of the time, that you embrace when you're willing to be open to all the possibilities.

I do what I do because it fills a need in me and gives me pleasure. When I dread the research, I'm able to overcome that dread through the promise that my research will pay off by helping me make a better novel, which gives me happiness. Life is too short to struggle in pain and in vain; my struggle is my opportunity, not my demise.

The student of novel writing must know, deep within, that this pursuit is meeting a need, bringing positive personal change, and providing a growing benefit to the person you are. Now, if you still think you want to be a novelist, do these things:

Be willing to work and study very, very hard.

Give yourself plenty of time.

Make sure you're doing what you want to do.

Open yourself up to every possibility.

Eschew gimmicks to get in print and focus your energy on becoming the best writer you can become.

Good luck. I wish you well; I wish you happiness.

Index

A

Ackroyd, Dan, 15
action-adventure novel, 8, 22, 118
action oriented plot, 82
... *And Ladies of the Club*, 23
"anticipated" conflict, 49
Antichrist, 57-58, 69
"Aunt Martha Syndrome, The," 86

B

balance of information, 91-92, 97
Beloved, 20
Bond, James, 42-43, 67, 104
book clubs, 125-26
Book of the Month Club, The, 126
building tension, 53, 100, 105, 128

C

Carnegie Hall, 10
Casablanca, 14
category romance, 8, 10, 36
central conflict, 48, 100
character growth, 32
character's voice, 75-76
Chelynne, 16
Clancy, Tom, 42, 94
Color Purple, The, 13, 20
coming of age novel, 8
Confederacy of Dunces, A, 20
Confessions of Nat Turner, The, 20
conflict. *See* central conflict
Cook, Robin, 8
Conroy, Pat, 134
crime stories, 9
Csikszentmihalyi, Mihalyi, 123

D

depth of character, 28
developing objectivity, 106
Donnelly, Frances, 61
Doubleday Book Club, 126
drop-dead line, 86, 134, 136

E

execution of technique, 127-28

F

Fancy Pants, 40
fanzines, 125
Firm, The, 83
first person point of view, 63-64
Flow: The Psychology of Optimal Experience, 123
Foreign Affairs, 20
freelance critique services 119-20

G

Gardner, John, 3, 105-06, 114
genre clubs, 126
Gone With the Wind, 18, 44, 49
Grafton, Sue, 139
Great American Novel, The, 10

H

Handmaid's Tale, The, 23
Hellion, The, 42
historical romance, 8, 13, 16, 18, 23, 118
History Book Club, The, 126
Hoffman, Alice, 33-34

Seventh Heaven, 33
Shake Down the Stars, 61
Sheppard, Jackie, 110-11, 113-14
Sleeping With the Enemy, 73
Sophie's Choice, 20
Spencer, LaVyrle, 42
Stout, David, 57
subplot, 46, 53-54, 100, 112, 116, 128, 131-32
Swain, Dwight V., 3, 50, 127

T

technique. *See* execution of technique
Techniques of the Selling Writer, 3, 50
techno-hero, 49, 51, 54, 57-58, 96, 115
techno-thriller, 8, 13-14, 16, 22, 27, 59, 95, 101, 104, 134, 139
Terms of Endearment, 15

third-person multiple point of view, 63-64
third-person subjective, 64
time line, 111-12
time-travel novel, 60
To Kill a Mockingbird, 20
tracking the plot, 112

V

value system, 38-39
vital need rule, 45-46
Vonnegut, Kurt, 63

W

Wambaugh, Joseph, 8-9
"whodunits," 22
Wingo, Tom, 87
Woman's Own, 23, 131
women's fiction, 23
Writer's Digest School, 2
writer's groups, 9
writer's style, 101-03

Other Books of Interest

Annual Market Books

Children's Writer's & Illustrator's Market, edited by Lisa Carpenter (paper) $17.95
Guide to Literary Agents & Art/Photo Reps, edited by Robin Gee $15.95
Novel & Short Story Writer's Market, edited by Robin Gee (paper) $19.95
Writer's Market, edited by Mark Kissling $25.95

General Writing Books

Beginning Writer's Answer Book, edited by Kirk Polking (paper) $13.95
Discovering the Writer Within, by Bruce Ballenger & Barry Lane $17.95
Freeing Your Creativity, by Marshall Cook $17.95
How to Write a Book Proposal, by Michael Larsen $11.95
Make Your Words Work, by Gary Provost $17.95
The 28 Biggest Writing Blunders, by William Noble $12.95
The Writer's Book of Checklists, by Scott Edelstein $16.95
The Writer's Digest Guide to Manuscript Formats, by Buchman & Groves $18.95
The Writer's Essential Desk Reference, edited by Glenda Neff $19.95

Fiction Writing

Characters & Viewpoint, by Orson Scott Card $13.95
The Complete Guide to Writing Fiction, by Barnaby Conrad $18.95
Cosmic Critiques: How & Why 10 Science Fiction Stories Work, edited by Asimov & Greenberg (paper) $12.95
Creating Characters: How To Build Story People, by Dwight V. Swain $16.95
Dialogue, by Lewis Turco $13.95
The Fiction Writer's Silent Partner, by Martin Roth $19.95
Handbook of Short Story Writing: Vol 1, by Dickson and Smythe (paper) $12.95
Handbook of Short Story Writing: Vol. II, edited by Jean Fredette (paper) $12.95
Manuscript Submission, by Scott Edelstein $13.95
Mastering Fiction Writing, by Kit Reed $18.95
Plot, by Ansen Dibell $13.95
Theme & Strategy, by Ronald B. Tobias $13.95
The 38 Most Common Fiction Writing Mistakes, by Jack M. Bickham $12.95
Writer's Digest Handbook of Novel Writing, $18.95
Writing the Novel: From Plot to Print, by Lawrence Block (paper) $11.95

Special Interest Writing Books

Armed & Dangerous: A Writer's Guide to Weapons, by Michael Newton (paper) $14.95
Deadly Doses: A Writer's Guide to Poisons, by Serita Deborah Stevens with Anne Klarner (paper) $16.95
Hillary Waugh's Guide to Mysteries & Mystery Writing, by Hillary Waugh $19.95
How to Write & Sell True Crime, by Gary Provost $17.95
How to Write Mysteries, by Shannon OCork $13.95
How to Write Science Fiction & Fantasy, Orson Scott Card $13.95
How to Write Tales of Horror, Fantasy & Science Fiction, edited by J.N. Williamson (paper) $12.95
Successful Scriptwriting, by Jurgen Wolff & Kerry Cox (paper) $14.95
The Writer's Complete Crime Reference Book, by Martin Roth $19.95
Writing the Modern Mystery, by Barbara Norville (paper) $12.95
The Writer's Guide to Self-Promotion & Publicity, by Elane Feldman $16.95
Writing A to Z, edited by Kirk Polking $24.95

To order directly from the publisher, include $3.00 postage and handling for 1 book and $1.00 for each additional book. Allow 30 days for delivery.

Writer's Digest Books, 1507 Dana Avenue, Cincinnati, Ohio 45207
Credit card orders call TOLL-FREE
1-800-289-0963
Prices subject to change without notice.

Write to this same address for information on *Writer's Digest* magazine, *Story* magazine, Writer's Digest Book Club, Writer's Digest School, and Writer's Digest Criticism Service.